D0213719

Thomas Hamm

James II and English Politics, 1678–1688

IN THE SAME SERIES

General Editors: Eric J. Evans and P.D. King

LANCASTER PAMPHLETS

James II and English Politics, 1678–1688

Michael Mullett

London and New York

First published in 1994
by Routledge
11 New Fetter Lane, London EC4P 4EE

Simultaneously published in the USA and Canada
by Routledge
29 West 35th Street, New York, NY 10001

© 1994 Michael Mullett

Typeset in 10 on 12pt Bembo by
Ponting–Green Publishing Services, Chesham, Bucks
Printed and bound in Great Britain by
Clays Ltd, St Ives plc

Printed on acid free paper

All rights reserved. No part of this book may be reprinted
or reproduced or utilized in any form or by any electronic,
mechanical, or other means, now known or hereafter
invented, including photocopying and recording, or in any
information storage or retrieval system, without
permission in writing from the publishers.

British Library Cataloguing in Publication Data
A catalogue record for this book is available from the British Library

Library of Congress Cataloging in Publication Data
Mullett, Michael
James II and English Politics, 1678–1688/Michael Mullett
p. cm. – (Lancaster pamphlets)
Includes bibliographical references
I. Title. II. Series.
BR756.D665 1994
274.2'06–dc20   93–19320

ISBN 0–415–09042–3

For Bishop B. C. Foley

Contents

Foreword

Lancaster Pamphlets offer concise and up-to-date accounts of major historical topics, primarily for the help of students preparing for Advanced Level examinations, though they should also be of value to those pursuing introductory courses in universities and other institutions of higher education. Without being all-embracing, their aims are to bring some of the central themes or problems confronting students and teachers into sharper focus than the textbook writer can hope to do; to provide the reader with some of the results of recent research which the textbook may not embody; and to stimulate thought about the whole interpretation of the topic under discussion.

Chronology of events

1678

August	Oates and Tonge present their testimony to Charles II
October	Coleman's papers examined; Godfrey's body discovered; Montagu testifies
November	Coleman tried and sentenced; Oates accuses the queen of planning to murder Charles
December	Coleman executed; impeachment of Danby launched

1679

January	Cavalier Parliament dissolved
March	Duke of York exiled; first Exclusion Parliament meets; Danby dismissed
April	Charles reconstructs privy council
May	bill of Exclusion passes the Commons; king prorogues parliament
July	Parliament dissolved
August	Charles falls ill
August–September	general election
September	York returns

October	Parliament meets and is prorogued; Shaftesbury dismissed from privy council; York leaves for Scotland; Monmouth dismissed

1680

January	York returns to England
June	York presented as a 'popish recusant'
October	following 'petitions' and recurrent prorogations, second Exclusion Parliament sits; vote for the bill of Exclusion, which is rejected by the Lords

1681

January	second Exclusion Parliament prorogued, then dissolved
February–March	general election
March	third Exclusion Parliament sits and is dissolved.
April	King's declaration published; Charles's agreement with Louis XIV
July	Shaftesbury arrested
November	Shaftesbury acquitted; *Absalom and Achitophel* published
December	trial of London's charter begins

1682

March	York returns to England
September	Monmouth undertakes 'progress' and is arrested
November	Shaftesbury flees to Holland

1683

January	death of Shaftesbury
June	*quo warranto* against London completed; disclosures of Rye House Plot

1685

February	Charles dies, James accedes
May	Parliament meets
June	Monmouth invades
July	Monmouth defeated at Sedgemoor
November	Parliament prorogued

1686

June	Godden v. Hales – verdict in favour of the dispensing power
July	appointment of Commissioners for Ecclesiastical Causes
September	Compton suspended

1687

April	first Declaration of Indulgence; campaign against Magdalen begins
July	Parliament dissolved
August–September	James on 'election tour'
October	James's 'three questions' issued

1688

April	second Declaration of Indulgence
May	petition of the seven bishops
June	acquittal of seven bishops; birth of Prince of Wales; letter of invitation to Orange
November	Orange lands; James retreats at Salisbury
December	James leaves England

1

Introduction: popery and politics

In 1688 King James II, like his brother and predecessor Charles II at his restoration to the throne in 1660, assumed the crown in circumstances of exceptional promise. The country was in the grip of a royalist reaction, and the parliament called for the new king's accession reflected this mood. Two insurrections in 1685 had the effect of deepening a loyalist swing in James's favour. However, less than four years later, James had thrown away all this bright legacy and was driven into abdication. His brother Charles had for the most part a difficult and at times stormy reign but had survived as monarch for twenty-five years and died a king. So how, in contrast with his royal brother, did James manage to terminate this own reign so abruptly?

The answer may lie in part in James's character. As well as being dignified, soldierly and regal, he was humourless, arrogant, obstinate, sometimes cruel, hectoring, brusque and unintelligent. As with many of his Stuart family, James's personality seems to have deteriorated as he grew older, and, as Dr Ashley wrote, the dashing soldier of his youth turned into the disagreeable prince of his middle years. However, in themselves the king's character traits would not have brought about his downfall; indeed, many actually admired the kingliness of James's imperious character. The real damage was done by the way that James II's domineering nature in pursuit of radical policies aroused the most antagonistic complex of religious and political feelings in the hearts of his fellow-countrymen, the feelings summed up in the term 'anti-popery'.

What, then, was this anti-popery, this set of values and prejudices that brought about the speedy demise of a king whose reign had begun so auspiciously? Anti-popery was a web of English political and religious attitudes to the Roman Catholic Church, its beliefs, practices and personnel. Suspicion of the papacy, the headship on earth of the Roman Catholic Church, was already ingrained in English attitudes even before the Reformation. The dissident Oxford theologian John Wyclif (d. 1384) had thundered out against the Roman papacy in works such as *De Papa, Concerning the Pope*. The fourteenth-century acts of parliament known as *Praemunire* and *Provisors* had severely restricted Rome's rights over the Catholic Church in England. Hostility to the papacy's intervention in English affairs, like hatred of the French, had in fact been an integral part of the nation's self-discovery, of late-medieval England's awakening nationalism.

The Protestant Reformation of the sixteenth century re-inforced and gave doctrinal coherence to this accumulating anti-papalism. The pope himself became demonized into a figure of total depravity and cruelty, the 'Antichrist'. John Foxe's lengthy account of Catholic persecution of Protestants, *The Actes and Monuments of the Church*, universally known as the *Book of Martyrs* (first published in 1563 and regularly reprinted), formed a national history which confirmed the identification of English nationality with Protestantism and anti-popery.

On the more purely political level, Catholicism came to be regarded as highly objectionable. In Europe at large, Spain, England's chief foe for much of the reign of Queen Elizabeth during the second half of the sixteenth century, was the principal standard bearer of the militant Catholic counter-offensive against Protestantism known as the Counter-Reformation. The pope himself was viewed as a despot and, in a country largely committed to the ideals of monarchy under the law, Catholicism appeared to be linked to, and to support, arbitrary and absolute government – tyranny, along the lines of what English people saw as the unchecked Catholic monarchies of France and Spain. The close connection between Catholicism and despotism and their combined insidious threat to English liberty was the theme of a work that captured the growing anti-popery of the 1670s,

2

Andrew Marvell's *Account of the Growth of Popery and Arbitrary Government* (1677).

'Papists', too, especially the powerful order of priests known as the Society of Jesus, or Jesuits, founded in the sixteenth century, seemed pledged to a total Machiavellian ruthlessness in advancing the interests of the Roman Church, and appeared committed to the idea that the ends justify the means. Indeed, in the sixteenth century some Jesuit thinkers had developed the political theory of tyrannicide, according to which it was permissible to assassinate any ruler who stood in the way of the interests of the Catholic Church. This theory was seen as underlying acts of Catholic terrorism such as the notorious Gunpowder Conspiracy against James I of England in 1605 and it seemed to lend credibility to the allegation of a Catholic plot against England's Protestant system in 1678. Whether in the form of structured state violence, as in the highly repressive Catholic reaction under England's Queen Mary between 1553 and 1558, or in unofficial plots and deeds of blood, the Catholic campaign against Protestantism, above all against English Protestantism, was seen in English Protestant eyes as uniquely determined, cunning, malevolent and violent. To achieve their diabolical ends, papists had, it was widely believed, sown the seeds of civil war between Charles I and his subjects in 1642. And it was an Anglo-Protestant article of faith that the Romanists had set fire to London in the city's great fire of 1666. After the fire itself and the terrible damage it did to Europe's leading city, the diarist Samuel Pepys, not normally a credulous man, wrote of 'apprehensions . . . of the rest of the city to be burned and the Papists to cut our throats'. Fears of Catholic menace were expressed in the clearest and most hysterical tones in a political pamphlet of 1679, *An Appeal from the country to the city,* . . .:

> . . . fancy that amongst the distracted crowd you behold troops of Papists ravishing your wives and daughters, dashing your little children's brains out against the walls, plundering your houses and cutting your own throats, by the name of heretic dogs . . .

Alongside such fears of Catholicism as a threat to English lives, property, national identity and distinctive political institutions, we must not overlook a deep loathing that existed for

Catholicism as a religious system. England was, after all, a deeply committed Protestant society presided over by an unmistakably Protestant church and pledged to the doctrines of the Reformation which Catholics rejected out of hand. Catholics were believed to spurn the Bible, the bedrock of the Reformation. Their respect for images of Christ and the saints seemed tantamount to idolatry, and the high esteem in which they held Mary, Christ's mother, seemed to suggest that they thought of her as divine. Their sacrament of confession of sins was seen as giving priests excessive moral and even sexual power over their clients, while Catholics' belief that in the sacrament of holy communion they actually consumed Christ's flesh struck many English people as little short of obscene; the Catholic Mass was officially identified as idolatrous. Catholics were also believed to abandon their rights of conscience and judgment to the pope and their priests.

However, though overwhelmingly Protestant, seventeeth-century England had a significant, though not large, Catholic community of about 1.5 per cent of the overall population; it was unevenly distributed around the country, with a particular pocket in Lancashire, and was relatively strong in the gentry and the peerage. It is noteworthy that these Catholics – recusants, as they were know legally – were not the main targets of mass violence in the episodic crises of anti-popery under Charles II and James II. There were deaths, it is true, between 1678 and 1681 in an epidemic of anti-Catholic feeling, but there was no holocaust. This was because the target on these occasions was popery, which was partly a fantasy or myth, rather than actual English Catholic neighbours. 'Popery' was seen essentially as a foreign thing, an international and French-led assault on Englishness. As we shall see, in 1688 James II awoke a fear of popery – of a great popish plot masterminded in Rome and Paris, carried out by barbarous Irish and directed, in characteristically 'popish' arbitrary fashion, against England's religion, freedom and laws. That was why he fell.

2

The Popish Plot

The 1670s saw an intensification of English anti-popery. Louis XIV's France, stridently Catholic, was on the march in Europe and was committing systematic aggression in the Low Countries, threatening the Protestant Dutch Republic. Though it was actually illegal to suggest that Charles II – the son of a Catholic mother, the husband of a Catholic – was a papist, suspicions were rife that the court was open to Romanist influences. Such suspicions seemed amply confirmed in 1673 when the heir presumptive, the king's brother, James, Duke of York, was forced to resign the office of Lord High Admiral because of his refusal to comply with the new Test Act and abjure the Catholic doctrine of the Mass: James's Catholicism was now public knowledge. The Duke's highly unpopular Catholic marriage to the Italian Maria Beatrice of Modena in 1673 made his Catholic commitment even more obvious. Under the leadership of the foremost minister, the authoritarian-inclined Lord Treasurer, the Earl of Danby, the government seemed to be putting in place the militarist absolutism that was viewed as the necessary concomitant of 'popery'. In these tense circumstances, in the late summer of 1678 stories of what appeared to be a 'Popish Plot' began to leak out, disclosed by Titus Oates and Israel Tonge.

Titus Oates (1649–1705) was an ordained minister who had taken service as chaplain to the Protestants in the Duke of

5

Norfolk's Catholic household, a highly useful opening since it brought him into the heart of the recusant community, providing him with insider knowledge which was to bring him fame and fortune in the years of his ascendancy as an 'informer'. In 1677 Oates declared himself a Catholic. Plausibility was his stock in trade, and he managed so successfully to convince Catholic authorities of his sincerity that in 1677 he was admitted to the English College of Valladolid, a seminary for training priests. He was expelled but then managed to gain admission to the Jesuit academy at St Omers in Flanders. By now Oates knew enough about both the Catholic world and the Catholic underworld to present an apparently believable invention of a Catholic plot.

Oates's partner, Israel Tonge (*c.* 1621–80), was a deranged cleric who dabbled in chemistry and made a living translating tracts by anti-Jesuit writers. In 1675 he was said to have heard of a plot to murder the king and replace him with James, and in 1676 he met Oates. In August 1678, using as an intermediary one Kirkby, a chemist known to the king through his own amateur interest in chemistry, Oates and Tonge were ready to present their story to Charles II.

The Oates–Tonge plot was a variant of the Catholic conspiracy genre that flourished in seventeenth-century England. Initially, Charles took little notice of this hackneyed testimony and left the matter in the hands of the privy council. In the original forty-three-clause deposition, James was not implicated – indeed, he, along with the king, was presented as the intended victim of a Catholic stratagem. But James was dragged into the plot when Oates, on 28 September, told the privy council that the papers of James's former secretary, Edward Coleman, might yield up interesting information. With the search of Coleman's lodgings, at the Earl of Danby's proposal, Oates struck gold. The secretary, a Catholic convert, had been in correspondence in 1674–5 not only with Louis XIV's confessor, Père la Chaise, but also with the papal internuncio in Brussels, and in his letters, which the privy council began reading early in October, Coleman had rashly written to express his hopes to reverse the Reformation and reconvert England 'which has for a long time been oppressed and miserably harassed with heresy and schism'. On 2 October parliament resumed and the investigation of Coleman was taken up. On 27 November he was tried for high treason and found

6

guilty as charged. The Lord Chief Justice presiding summed up: 'Mr Coleman, your own papers are enough to condemn you' (though his 'own papers' did not condemn him of the specific plot alleged by Oates and Tonge) and he was executed on 3 December by hanging, drawing and quartering.

Was James implicated in Coleman's machinations? John Miller writes that 'Coleman's letters placed [James] squarely in the centre' of Oates's plot; he suggests that the Duke had to struggle hard 'to avoid being dragged down with' Coleman, and was let off the hook by the House of Lords' deferential preparedness to accept his word as a prince. F. C. Turner, James's standard biographer, went even further and claimed that James was 'sufficiently responsible for the content of Coleman's letters to be seriously implicated in Coleman's guilt'. A highly revealing letter from the Duke to Coleman's correspondent Père la Chaise – and from the very same period when Coleman was involved in his manoeuvres – suggests that the secretary enjoyed York's complete trust; the Duke refers to Coleman as 'one of my family [household] in whom I have great confidence'. Fortunately for the Duke, such material was not available to parliament in the autumn of 1678. However, the Coleman scandal encouraged the belief that, for as long as James remained both a Catholic and heir presumptive, Catholic extremists such as Coleman, pinning their hopes on the Duke's faith, would continue with their schemes, and that therefore, in part for his own good and certainly for the good of the nation, the Duke should be at least distanced from the king and perhaps cut off from the line of succession. Thus a kind of conservative movement against James grew up – or rather, not against James in person but designed to protect him, the king and the country from the consequences of his being Catholic in so far as his religion, whatever his own expressed wishes, encouraged Catholic extremists. Various members of parliament spoke of their 'extreme veneration for the Duke' but of their alarm at 'his being next of blood to the succession of the crown, and what encouragement that may give the Papists to take away the King' and of 'the hopes the Papists have of the Duke's religion'.

At this stage, then, a prevalent mood was one of seeing James, merely by being a Catholic, as innocently responsible, so to speak, for Catholic conspiracy. Yet people seemed to know that it was futile to try to de-convert the obstinate James. Thus it was

7

coming to be perceived that all that could be done in terms of neutralizing the Duke's passive menace as popish successor was to debar him from the succession. That was the genesis of 'Exclusion', though, as we shall see, some went beyond the position that the Duke was only a passive victim of a conspiracy going on around him without his consent.

The Coleman case was not the only sensational event of the autumn of 1678; another, which seemingly provided further proof of the limitless malevolence and violence of 'papists', was the mysterious death of Sir Edmund Berry Godfrey. Godfrey, a prosperous London timber merchant and Justice of the Peace, had played a hero's role during the plague in London in 1665. As a magistrate, he was kindly disposed towards Nonconformists and easy on Catholics; his acquaintances included Edward Coleman. A tribute to him by the contemporary historian Bishop Gilbert Burnet brings out his tolerant spirit:

> A zealous Protestant he was, and a true lover of the Church of England, but he had kind thoughts of the Nonconformists, was not forward to execute the laws against them, and, to avoid doing that, was not apt to search for priests or mass houses, so that few men of the like zeal lived on better terms with the Papists than he.

On 6 September 1678, in his capacity as a Justice of the Peace, Godfrey took down a sworn statement to the effect that information in the possession of Oates, Tonge and Kirkby was true. Then, towards the end of the month, Oates left with Godfrey a copy of his actual paper of information. Godfrey now seems to have realized that, as legal custodian of Oates's testimony, he was in a highly exposed position and was supposed to have exclaimed, 'Upon my conscience, I shall be the first martyr.' Furthermore, Godfrey also held a long conversation with Edward Coleman and was reported to have found Oates 'sworn and . . . perjured' – though in testimony at his inquest it was alleged that Godfrey had 'believed that surely there was a plot'.

At 9 o'clock on the morning of Saturday 12 October Godfrey left his Charing Cross home and was possibly seen several times during the course of the day, in or near the Strand. He then went missing for five days until, on the evening of 17 October, his body was found in a ditch on far-away Primrose Hill, near Hampstead.

An inquest was held the next day and went into considerable anatomical detail, as reported by a secretary of state:

Sir E. Godfrey.

The coroner came in and gave account of the view of the body. NB – The hilt of the sword was three inches from the ground. No blood near the place nor where the body was, none under the hilt of the sword. A bruise on the top of the breast just under the collar. A circle round his neck like those that are strangled. . . . His shoes, the soles extreme clean. No dry dirt on them. His body did stink. Faces [faeces?] redder than ordinary [?], therefore not dead of wounds, which would make them pale. . . . His neck turned all one way to the left. His eyes closed and his mouth. Extreme empty – therefore had not eaten in two days or more.

These are various forensic constructions we can put upon the coroner's reports. One highly likely interpretation is that Godfrey was not stabbed to death. (Dead bodies do not bleed.) Some bruising, contortions around the neck and head and the absence of food in the cadaver may suggest some brutal treatment in captivity before death. There is clear evidence of strangulation, either by others or as a suicide by hanging. The death did not occur at the place of discovery of the corpse, and the body, which had expired some time before, probably at the weekend ('his body did stink'), had been taken to Primrose Hill between Tuesday, when a visitor to the site had seen nothing untoward, and Thursday. Several circumstances pointed to a person or persons trying deliberately, if not always very knowledgeably or skilfully, to confuse any straightforward forensic investigation.

It is hardly surprising that Godrey's death has aroused intense speculation on the part of historians and crime writers down to the present day. There are so many missing pieces in this jigsaw, so many conflicting statements, and anomalies like the Protestant magistrate's friendship with the fanatical Catholic secretary, Coleman. A fascinating summary of the case can be read in the appendix to John Kenyon's *The Popish Plot* (1972).

One possibility is that Godfrey, a melancholic, the balance of whose mind may have been tipped by receiving Oates's testimony, committed suicide by hanging himself. He was a rich businessman and unmarried. As the law then stood, the estate of a suicide was forfeit to the crown and it is alleged that his legal heirs sought to conceal the fact of suicide by faking a stabbing. Other hypotheses are suggested: that Godfrey, once foreman of a jury that had brought in a guilty verdict against a noble homicidal maniac, was the victim of a revenge killing by the lethal aristocrat; that Oates killed Godfrey, or had him killed, to vindicate his testimony; and that James or his agents were the guilty parties because Coleman had told Godfrey about a secret Jesuit conference in the Duke's apartment, so that the magistrate knew too much to be allowed to live.

These are all intriguing pieces of detective guesswork but it seems unlikely now that any of them can ever be proved. At the time, though, only one conclusion seemed possible: Godfrey was murdered by Jesuits, fitting in with the order's image of ruthless violence. The normally judicious diarist John Evelyn, generally sceptical about Oates, assumed that this was a Catholic assassination – 'The murder of Sir Edmundbury Godfrey . . . as was manifest by the Papists . . .' – while the sober Nonconformist Richard Baxter thought that Godfrey's murder proved Oates's testimony.

Oates was now indeed on the crest of a wave, and to cast doubt on his 'evidence' was itself taken as evidence of popish predilections. On 15 November, buoyed up with his own recent successes, Oates overstepped the mark in accusing Charles II's 'pious and vertuous' [Evelyn] Portuguese Catholic wife of planning to poison the king. Despite this indiscretion, Oates still possessed extraordinary public credibility. His testimony was responsible for the impeachement (a trial for one's life in parliament) on 15 November of five leading Catholic peers including the seventy-two-year-old Lord Arundell of Wardour, whom Oates identified as intended first minister in an imposed Roman Catholic regime, and John Baron Bellasis, aged sixty-four, whom he named as captain-general of the Romanist army of invasion.

The presence of such individuals on Oates's list indicates the continued strength of Catholics in the peerage, and there were also fears about the possible presence of Catholics in the House of Commons. To deal with this perceived problem, parliament now passed a second Test Act which laid down qualifications by oath for membership of either house of parliament, probed into a whole range of Catholic beliefs about the Mass and the saints and required the swearer not only to *re*nounce these beliefs but to *de*nounce them as 'superstitious and idolatrous'.

Taking precedence in the secular nobility and with the right to sit in the Lords was the Duke of York. How, as a peer and a devout Catholic, did the new Test Act affect him? By the narrowest majority, York was exempted from the statute with the proviso clause: 'Provided always that nothing in the Act contained shall extend to his royal Highness the duke of York.' A move to debar York from parliament – to exclude him – might easily have made a precedent for a more ambitious scheme to keep him out of the succession. For the moment such plans were in abeyance.

As the autumn proceeded, it was the Earl of Danby who bore the brunt of attacks from the opposition in parliament. In foreign policy, Charles II was strongly inclined to ally with France and it was with only the greatest difficulty that Danby was able to persuade him to adopt the 'patriotic' policy of alliance with Protestant Holland against France. In fact, earlier in 1678, Charles had broken free from Danby's anti-French, pro-Dutch line in foreign policy; for a bribe of £450,000 from Louis XIV, the king had agreed to prorogue (postpone the sitting of) his anti-French parliament, stand down the army raised to halt French aggression in the Low Countries and lean on the Dutch Republic to accept France's surrender terms. On Charles's direct instructions, Danby wrote to the English ambassador in Paris, Ralph Montagu, to enquire about the sending of the money. Danby was acting here against his own principles of policy but, as the king's minister, was obliged to write as he did. By October ambassador Montagu, with a personal grievance against Danby and prompted by Louis XIV, had broadcast the contents of the correspondence to the Commons.

What were Louis XIV's motives in all this? The French king was determined to foment as much discord as he could in England, to keep his cousin Charles weak and to neutralize the once feared English as a force in Europe. In particular, and with fine irony, Louis set out to bring down the anti-French Danby by means of releasing documents that showed him to have sold out Holland and advanced the interest of France. By 21 December the House of Commons had prepared articles of impeachment against Danby, concentrating on the alleged offences under the heading of foreign policy and claiming that the minister had carved out a pro-French policy of his own – regardless of the fact that the Montagu letters were written at the personal direction of Danby's royal master.

By now English politics had reached an extremely complex and dangerous stage. Opposition members of parliament, some of whom were in receipt of French bribes paid to encourage them to attack the anti-French Lord Treasurer, were pursuing charges against him that could surely end only in blood. Danby, however, was not made of the stuff of martyrs: had the hunt against him continued, he would undoubtedly have revealed that he had acted at the king's behest – with incalculable consequences for the monarchy. For some time, oppositionists, led by Anthony Ashley Cooper, Earl of Shaftesbury, had been arguing that the very continuance of the 'Cavalier' Parliament, first elected in 1661 and still providing Danby with a measure of support, was illegal since it was in breach of the 1664 Triennial Act (calling for a parliament every three years). Voices calling for a dissolution were now joined by that of the Lord Treasurer himself, desperate to save his skin. On 24 January 1679 Charles finally dissolved his long parliament. This new year would bring parliamentary elections amidst an anti-popish panic that showed no signs of abating.

3

Exclusion

From the beginning of 1679 Charles II exerted himself, and he became the central coordinator of policy in the crucial subsequent two and a half years. The energy that the king had for so long channelled into pleasure-seeking was now redirected into a political management approaching statesmanship, with Charles giving a glimpse of the kind of king he might have been had he applied himself.

The dissolution of the Cavalier Parliament has to be seen as a device to buy a little time rather than as a way of killing the pursuit of Danby or of James. The court had no reason to hope for favourable results from the general election held early in the new year. The well-informed French ambassador estimated that the strength of the court 'party' in the Commons would not rise above fifty. Yet that was pessimistic. The Earl of Shaftesbury, who now began building the first organized English parliamentary political party, calculated that the court would be able to muster 158 firm supporters – by no means a derisory figure – against his opposition's 302. However, the most striking fact about the membership of the new House of Commons was its political inscrutability. Half the members of the new House consisted of new men without a parliamentary record, and Shaftesbury, who prided himself on his detailed information, put down thirty-six members as 'doubtful' that is, politically unpredictable. In addition, Shaftesbury's own figures on voting

13

support were optimistic. Himself the most partisan of men, he seriously underestimated the large number of MPs who would abstain in even the most epoch-making votes. The typical back-bencher of this period – an unpaid amateur representing the interest of his local community – was not always well informed but looked for reassurance, sought guidance, respected the crown and was suspicious of the court, upheld the Church of England and demanded guarantees against 'popery'.

Measures taken by the king in the early months of 1679 were designed to reassure new and inexperienced members and the non-partisans who held the key to the situation. In the first place, James had to be got out of the country. Charles expelled James for two reasons. First, the king had to think long and hard, and the presence of James, who was always prone to think in terms of extremist and militarist solutions, was not conducive to cool thought. Second, the king was seeking to win over the moderate and uncertain members of parliament in offering guarantees against popery by removing the man in whom, it was believed, papist plotters had been placing their hopes. With the parliament about to convene on 21 March 1679, Charles ordered the Duke to depart the realm. James was most unwilling to comply. He felt that he was the best defender of his own endangered interests in the country and that while he was out of England his hand in the game would not be played. Moreover, James believed that during his absence his brother, whom he revered as king but whom he thought lacking in firmness, would capitulate to the opposition, thereby becoming no more than a titular king. For James, however, the absolute obedience due to divine-right monarchy was no mere abstract doctrine but a central principle of personal conduct, so that on 3 March 1679 he and his Duchess left England for the Low Countries. But before leaving James extracted an important concession. Lest his interest in the succession be sacrificed to that of the king's eldest illegitimate son, the Duke of Monmouth, he successfully insisted on an official declaration from Charles, in the privy council, that Monmouth was indisputably illegitimate and thus disqualified from succeeding. Richard Baxter neatly summed up the situation: 'The Duke of York . . . removed out of England, by the king's command; who yet stands to maintain his succession.'

Charles had gained a little breathing space for James and

himself, but the prosecution of Danby was now resumed with gusto. His case involved two important issues of legal and constitutional principle. The first of these turned on whether or not the bishops could vote in capital cases in the House of Lords in its capacity as a high court of justice to try peers such as Danby. Given the small numerical size of their lordships' House, the presence of the bishops could make a crucial difference to the outcome of a vote on Danby's guilt or innocence. The issue occasioned a disagreement between the Lords and the Commons. But one particular insight can be gained from this dispute: in the tug-of-war over the bishops' voting, it was generally recognized that, as loyal Churchmen, crown appointees and believers in the Anglican doctrine of divine-right monarchy (albeit sometimes critical of individual policies), the bishops could be relied upon in a crisis to cast their votes overwhelmingly for the crown – and, more immediately, for the Anglican statesman Danby. The support of the Church was to prove indispensable to the crown in weathering the storms of 1679–81 and in rebuilding its authority thereafter.

The second issue of legal and constitutional import, one with wide implications for the future, was that of the scope of royal pardons. Charles dismissed the Lord Treasurer with effect from 25 March 1679, but any trial would almost certainly uncover the king's complicity with France at a time when the nation was supposed to be engaged against her. Therefore, Charles suppressed the trial by pardoning the Earl. The use of the pardon infuriated the Commons. In addresses and resolutions, the House, 'come up to demand Judgement in their own Names, and the Names of all the Commons of *England*, against *Thomas*, Earl of *Danby*', claimed – though without any effect – that the royal pardon he pleaded in bar of an impeachment was 'illegal and void' and ought not to be so pleaded.

The debate, which crystallized the whole issue, so vital for the future of the constitution, of the answerability of ministers – whether to parliament or to the crown – was not pursued. Thwarted over impeachment, the Commons took another tack, an act of attainder, a measure simply declaring the guilt of the accused to be a fact. When this process was almost complete, the Earl suddenly gave himself up, and was brought to the bar of the House of Lords to be apprised of his rights in law: 'So he withdrew, and was by order of the house committed to the

Tower.' There the matter rested and Danby, so recently the most powerful politician in England, was to spend the next five years – a period of unrivalled political excitement – in by no means uncomfortable imprisonment.

Letting Danby off the hook was not a measure particularly designed to placate the moderates. However, a further step taken by Charles in April was supremely conciliatory as well as vastly skilful. The king himself announced this measure in April in a speech to both Houses:

My Lords and Gentlemen: I thought it requisite to acquaint you with what I have done now this day; which is, that I have established a new Privy Council, the constant number of which shall never exceed thirty. I have made choice of such men as are worthy and able to advise me; and am resolved, in all my weighty and important affairs, next to the advice of my Great Council in Parliament (which I shall very often consult with) to be advised by this Privy Council.

The king was here drawing parliament's attention to the reconstruction of the privy council, the highest organ of state under the crown, into a smaller and more efficient version of this body. In deferring to the notion of an effective privy council Charles was, seemingly, falling in with long-standing constitutionalist principles. Here in the privy council was the ideal of open government by the magnates and foremost public servants, all fearlessly giving the sovereign the kind of frank advice the realm needed – the antithesis of the secretive and self-seeking caballing of mistresses and favourites that Charles was said to favour as a mode of government. Charles announced the reform in his April speech in his usual suave and gracious tones, so unlike his brother's soldierly and staccato bluster. With more than a hint of turning over a new leaf, what Charles was saying in his April address was that he was now taking parliament fully into his confidence and that the new privy council was the seal of this new relationship – both highly reassuring messages.

However, the rebuilding of the privy council was all so much legerdemain – in Professor Jones's words, 'the king's first move in his bid to wrest the initiative from the Whigs'. Typical of the king's strategy was the appointment as lord president of the council of the opposition's presiding genius and James's undying foe, the Earl of Shaftesbury, alongside another noble captain of opposition, Arthur Capel, Earl of Essex. These promotions were in fact illusions. For one thing, continuing governmental evolution had made the privy council largely an anachronism. Effective governance in late Stuart England was conducted in small specialist committees and boards, by experts, rather than by senates of barons. The privy council as an institution was now well advanced in its long-term slide into decorative irrelevance, while the office of its lord president was an empty title which certainly gave its holder no entrée into the king's confidence. Charles's remark to a loyalist peer, – 'god's fish, they have put a set of men about me, but they shall know nothing' – reveals the king's intention of deceiving the opposition with a mere show of power. Yet by seeming to take oppositionists into his government and confidence, Charles was seriously weakening them as adversaries. Wavering public opinion would conclude from these promotions that the noise the opposition made over popery and the succession was so much bluster, cynically used to pressure their way into office. In addition, through seemingly buying out the leaders of his critics, Charles was severing them from their grass-roots support in the electorate, in London, amongst the strongly anti-Catholic Nonconformists and in parliament. The rank and file of the court's opponents showed such distrust of the leadership at this stage that on 1 May a test bill was introduced in the Commons requiring by-elections for all members accepting office under the crown. These were important gains for Charles – division amongst his opponents and the discrediting of their leaders – and all won at minimal political cost to him.

J. R. Jones (1970) points to a 'serious crisis' in May 1679 for the opposition, demoralized as a result of the king's coup. However, if the opposition was in crisis, the court's propects in the spring and early summer of 1679 seemed dismal, even to some of its steadiest supporters. Sir John Reresby, York's dependent, reported: 'At this time, the state of the kingdom and government looked very melancholy. The king was poor; there was not money sufficient for bread for the King's family.' Evelyn observed that 'there was a sad prospect of public affairs'. At the root of the trouble was the mounting onslaught on the Duke of York. In parliament, after a radical London MP had gone so far as to propose the impeachment of the Duke for high treason, a resolution was adopted in April: 'That the Duke of York being a Papist and the hopes of his coming to the Crown hath given the greatest countenance and encouragement to the present conspiracies and designs of the Papists against the King and the Protestant Religion.'

The ambiguity, deliberate or accidental, in the motion over whether it was York, being a papist, who fomented Catholic plotting or whether York's simply being a Catholic encouraged Catholics to intrigue, without his consent, was resolved by the royalist-dominated House of Lords which inserted into the Commons motion the crucial modifying adverb 'unwittingly': 'Hath unwittingly given the greatest countenance . . .'. In a sense, though, it hardly mattered: whether or not York, passively or actively, wittingly or un-wittingly, gave rise to extremist designs, his Catholicism and his status as heir to the throne could still be perceived as having a profoundly destabilizing effect, and many now believed that effect would not disappear until York's ineradicable Cath-olicism and his position as successor were separated. Others were aware of an even deeper problem: plot or no plot, York was still scheduled to succeed his brother and the nation would then, through the normal course of succession, be confronted with a popish regime.

Thus pressure mounted to change those ground rules of succession by specifying an absolute exclusion of the Duke from the inheritance to the throne. (No provision was made for James's reverting to Protestantism.) On 15 May the loyalist element in the Commons, seeing the way the wind was blowing and afraid to expose their own numerical weakness, backed down from forcing a division on the first reading of a bill to exclude the Duke. At second reading, on 21 May, the bill went through by a majority of 207 to 128. On the grounds of a dispute between the two Houses over the procedure to be used in the Danby trial (see above, p. 15), the king killed the bill, first by proroguing parliament on 26 May and then, some weeks later, by proclamation dissolving parliament and issuing writs for new elections. The judicious use of these powers of pro-rogation and dissolution, more than any other single 'consti-tutional' factor, allowed Charles II to weather and eventually to survive the storm of Exclusion.

We shall next consider, first, some of the patterns of voting on the bill of Exclusion, taking samples from the parliament of spring 1679; second, the bill's specific provisions; and third, its wider implications.

Considering that the three parliaments held between March 1679 and March 1681 are generally known as 'Exclusion parliaments', it is remarkable that only in the first of the series did the issue come to a Commons division. Also remarkable is the fact that in May 1679 out of 509 members only 335 actually voted. How is this to be explained? For one thing, it is likely that these failures to vote were not all a matter of negligence alone but rather a conscious choice. Before the key vote, sessions had been generally well attended and these were early days in the session, before debate fatigue could be expected to affect MPs – indeed, heavy pressure had been brought to bear on them to attend and vote. The way certain members from particular counties failed to vote in quite solid blocs confirms a feeling that abstention arose in many cases out of positive and careful choice and even collusion. What, in turn, might that indicate? It might suggest that, while many members remained fearful of James's Catholicism, they wanted to be shown ways of defusing the issue other than by the extreme course of Exclusion. Also, the decision *not* to vote may have been part of a reluctance to polarize parliament and the nation. Many members would have had in mind the history of the run-up to the civil war, when vote after vote in parliament had divided the community of the realm into two warring factions. For the king there was a possible constituency of supporters from amongst these admittedly anxious members who were still not prepared to vote in favour of Exclusion.

A further and related point is that only a minority of MPs actually wanted Exclusion badly enough to vote for it and that the majority, 302, were saying, either by voting against the bill or not voting, that they did not want it or had serious reservations about it. Exclusion did continue to have widespread popular support in the constituencies: 80 per cent of those who voted in favour were returned by their constituents in the next general election. However, there may have been a tendency for pro-Exclusionist popular opinion to run ahead of the views of significant numbers of members of parliament, recruited as these were from the ranks of the propertied and inclined in many cases to be suspicious of radical solutions. Charles needed to do two things at this delicate stage: reassure hesitant members

19

of the ruling class – the 'political nation' – and avoid antagonizing popular feeling. Both aims dictated that James be kept out
of the country. Hardly had the Duke left England than rumours
reported 'as if the duke of York was returning for England'.
Not only was James chafing at his enforced idleness in Brussels,
but he became alarmed at Charles's concessions, which he
regarded as a sell-out of the interests of the dynasty and the
monarchy. The king, however, had to keep him at arm's length.
When James wrote to Charles urging his own return and the
adoption of get-tough policies, the king firmly ordered him to
stay put in view of the 'temper of the people . . . in all places,
especially in London'.

Although, as we shall see, mass opinion, even in London,
was far from being uniformly hostile to James and his brand of
politics, the king was at this stage right to a large extent in
diagnosing an anti-York mood amongst the ordinary Londoners.
For instance, when the Duke did briefly 'come over' in the
summer, the London crowd shouted 'a Pope, a Pope' at his
retinue.

Having now considered the voting on the bill of Exclusion
and some of the political implications of the vote, we turn next
to examine the specific provisions of the measure.

The bill of Exclusion was an intended third Test Act, a
disqualificatory measure concerned with the religious criteria
for occupying a particular public office, that of king. In this
particular case, the would-be-office-holder had already failed
the religious test and, as his rejection of a recent high level
episcopal mission to re-convert him had shown, was an irreconcilable papist.

The Exclusion bill was concerned entirely with one individual, James, Duke of York, who was identified by name a
dozen times in the text. In this respect it differed from later
parliamentary measures, the bill of Rights of 1689 and the Act
of Settlement of 1701, which set out the general order of
succession to the throne. The three Exclusion bills of 1679–81,
by contrast, aimed not to debar categories of persons from, or
qualify them for, the succession, but only to disinherit one
individual, York, from it. The bills purported to do so not only
on the grounds that York's merely being a papist incited popish
conspiracy but also on the assumption that his succeeding
would in effect destroy Protestantism in England; he himself

20

was now unambiguously identified as a direct menace to the survival of Protestantism. The Exclusion bill did not simply set out to prevent York from succeeding. In a series of ferocious penal clauses, it promised death by hanging, drawing and quartering for York himself, should he assert his succession or even enter the realm, and for any who supported him, even to the extent of preaching or writing that he was the lawful successor. However, in taking preventive measures to avoid York's succeeding, with the aid of sympathizers, and in particular in indemnifying in advance all those who would 'in case of resistance fight and . . . by force . . . subdue' the Duke's supporters, the framers of the Exclusion bill were in effect sketching in a civil war scenario. The nation, however, still lived under the shadow of the terrible civil wars of the 1640s, and many drew back from a measure which actually made provision for civil war and which invited violence from York, not just in defence of his title but of his very life. In addition, the threat of death by bloody torture against a royal prince would have revolted many.

The Exclusionists certainly recognized that York had a following, which included his personal dependents, militant Roman Catholics and convinced monarchists and legitimists of all kinds. He also had supporters in Ireland and Scotland and throughout an overwhelmingly monarchist Europe, especially in mighty France. As Burnet put it:

> a total exclusion, . . . might provoke other princes to assist the Duke in the recovery of his right, might stir up many in England to espouse his cause, might encourage the Scotch, in hope of his future favour, to assert his title, and so kindle a war about us, as well as raise distractions at home.

With such support for James, the fear of civil war in the event of the enactment of Exclusion was high, though the certainty of the Exclusionists' winning such a war was not. James might well succeed after all; and if he did as a result of civil war, through rivers of blood with foreign armies on English soil, he would succeed as a vengeful conqueror. Moreover, he would have a free hand as a popish tyrant.

Amongst the other problems over Exclusion was a constitutional obstacle. The parliament through which the bills of Exclusion had to proceed was in fact a trinity made up of 'the

21

king, lords and commons in parliament assembled'. This meant that, in the first place, bills that had passed the Commons had also to clear to the Lords, whose assent could not in constitutional terms be taken for granted and whose overwhelming royalism, fortified by the presence of the bishops, would prove a formidable obstacle to Exclusion. In the second place, the royal assent in the seventeenth-century constitution was not automatic. Even in the unlikely event of an Exclusion bill's passing the Lords, if the king refused to consent the bill would fall at the last. Could Charles, then, be forced into accepting Exclusion? Constitutionally he could not, and politically he could be coerced into accepting the bill only if the Commons, which granted his revenue, could bring irresistible financial pressure to bear on him. However, the country was at peace and the army was scaled down. Peace abroad also allowed trade to recover, with customs receipts flowing into the Exchequer. The revenue, set at £1.2 million at the Restoration but for years never reaching that sum, had settled down by the mid-to late-1670s at anywhere between £1.3 and £1.4 million p.a. – sufficient, with an eye to economy, to cover peacetime needs.

Thus the House of Commons was in no position to blackmail King Charles financially into accepting Exclusion. He had no illusions about James or his limited intellect and poor judgment, but he was determined to stand by him. Charles was not normally a resolute man; he avoided rather than sought trouble. So why, and at such inconvenience to himself and his preference for a quiet life, was he so firm on James's right to succeed? Perhaps it was a matter of the clan solidarity of the restored Stuarts who felt that unless they hung together they would hang separately. Perhaps, too, Charles shared the fears of many of his subjects of a civil war following Exclusion, a conflict in which the monarchy and the monarch might once more perish. Charles had of course abandoned positions in the past. However, now approaching fifty, he was perceptibly hardening up and becoming more regal. He must have been aware that to surrender on the succession, effectively making England an elective monarchy, would turn the king into a derisory figurehead. Charles, then, had no intention of giving way on Exclusion and he may have calculated that if he stood firm the political odds were in his favour to win.

Exclusion was in many ways a flawed cause, but the most

serious defect in the actual bills introduced to enact it was their consistent failure to name an alternative successor to James. It was as if the designers of the Exclusion bills were so obsessed with York that they forgot to propose a replacement, except in the following woolly phrase, which created more problems than it solved:

the . . . crown shall descend to and be enjoyed by such person and persons successively during the lifetime of the said James, duke of York as should have inherited and enjoyed the same in case the said James, duke of York, were naturally dead.

James's own successor in the normal line of descent would have been his elder daughter Mary, married to William, Stadholder of Holland. However, it was unlikely that Mary would rule alone, so that England would be likely to be taking on Mary's formidable Dutch husband as king. A Dutchman! The seventeenth-century English loathed all foreigners, but they had fought three recent wars against the Dutch and had built up a whole lexicon of derision of the Netherlanders, depicting them as misers ('Dutch treat'), cowards and drunkards ('Dutch courage'). But if a Dutch king, with his well-known obsession with combating France, were not acceptable, what other choice was there? A possibility being canvassed quite extensively was that of Charles's illegitimate son, the Duke of Monmouth (1649–85).

Monmouth had undoubted star quality. Handsome and athletic, with a legacy of his father's easy affability, the young duke had all the requirements for a fantasy figure in popular culture, taking the lead role of the 'Protestant Duke', with York, the 'Popish Duke', cast as the wicked uncle. Heedlessly enough, Charles advanced Monmouth, thereby feeding speculation about the king's ultimate plans for him. Made captain-general in 1678, he achieved the pinnacle of his military fame by routing Scots rebels in the summer of 1679. Yet there was a growing distancing between Monmouth and his father. For Monmouth was overstepping the mark and, according to Reresby, 'was manifestly in the councils against the Duke his uncle'. Monmouth was in fact putting in a definite bid to displace York in the succession: to counter this, in March 1679 Charles solemnly declared that he had never married Monmouth's mother, and in September Monmouth was stripped of his captain-generalcy. Thus was set in motion the alienation between the senior Stuarts and the royal bastard that was to culminate in Monmouth's execution in 1685.

There were indeed serious doubts about Monmouth. Reresby hinted at the problem delicately enough: 'though the Duke of Monmouth was very handsome and accomplished as to his outside, his parts were not suitable'. The pen-portraitist Anthony Hamilton came right out and said it: 'he was greatly deficient in mental accomplishments'. A successor somewhat slow off the mark mentally would surely fall under the influence of more intelligent and manipulative politicians: would not a Monmouth kingship in effect be that of the Earl of Shaftesbury? At the same time, even had Monmouth been as mentally acute as he was physically graced, there remained a doubt not so much over his personality as over his person, as a bastard whose succession would break with precedent and law and set an ill example for the rights of legitimate inheritance of all titles and properties.

The failure to deal adequately with provisions for the succession were James to be debarred raised the most serious doubts about the basic wisdom of Exclusion; and the more this was looked at, the less it seemed the simple solution it might first have appeared to be. There was, however, an alternative remedy to James's popery that many, including, apparently, Charles, found acceptable: 'limitations', restricting the powers of a popish successor. On 30 April 1679 Charles himself set out the details of a scheme of limitations in a speech to the House of Lords: a Catholic successor's powers over the Church, the judiciary and the armed forces would all be severely restricted.

Two questions arise over the 'limitations' scheme: why did Charles offer them and would they have amounted to a workable option? Charles offered limitations largely to create an image of conciliation, continuing to aim for the middle ground of politics. At the same time, he must have been virtually sure that the opposition would throw out the plan – Burnet wrote that they 'laughed at it' – because they were aware that if James came to the throne, limited or not, he would be king and would have their heads as punishment for their designs against him. Knowing that the Exclusionists had to reject limitations, Charles could still force them into the politically unattractive posture of repudiating a royal compromise.

Aside from Charles's tactical motives in putting forward limitations, was the plan in itself workable? The answer must be no. For one thing, limitations threatened to do what Exclusion would bring about – make the English monarchy a titular state presidency. One version of the scheme envisaged James as king in name only, his powers exercised by a regent, perhaps the Prince of Orange. Surely, though, that was practically Exclusion by another name.

A fresh crisis in the summer of 1679 refocused attention on these questions of succession. Suddenly Charles succumbed to a grave illness, and leading ministers, understandably fearing the king's death and a coup by Monmouth, decided to recall the heir. James's return to London on 1 September was the beginning of a long, slow climb back to acceptance that would culminate in his triumphant accession in 1685.

What were James's and the crown's overall prospects in the second half of 1679? There were in fact some hesitant signs of recovery in the monarchy's fortunes. An overwhelmingly Exclusionist parliament was returned in the summer general election following dissolution in July, but after its first meeting on 7 October Charles held it at bay by successively proroguing it – in all eight times – until he finally allowed it to meet over a year later. Shaftesbury was dismissed from the lord presidency on 14 October and the balance of power between Monmouth and York swung in the latter's favour. Dismissed from his command, Monmouth was ordered abroad, whereas York was now permitted to stay in Britain, in Edinburgh. His slow progress to Scotland in the autumn had allowed observers to test opinion towards the Duke in the English provinces. There were no open shows of hostility and James secured the allegiance of important provincial power-brokers and of leading northern Churchmen. Even more impressive was James's reception in Scotland, not only by the aristocracy and gentry but among the common people too. James conducted himself with unwonted tact in Edinburgh and consolidated an important power base in Scotland.

If we review the underlying position of the crown within the political system at the end of 1679, we are struck by its fundamental solidity. Charles was deploying to good effect prerogative powers such as prorogation. The House of Common's prestige was dented by its obsession with a single issue and its comparative legislative inaction. The court had particular grounds for confidence when the situation in 1679 was contrasted with that which had prevailed back in 1641. At that time a bankrupt monarchy had to go cap in hand to a hostile parliament, while a series of secessionist rebellions in Scotland, and then in Ireland brought civil war ever nearer to England. Now, in 1679, the King's finances were reasonably sound, Ireland was at peace and Scotland, after the brief and easily suppressed flare-up of insurgency in the summer, was tranquil and, as James found, loyal.

Was Exclusionism doomed then? By no means. Yet parliament was the Exclusionists' forum and, with parliament in suspension for more than a year, the leaders of the opposition had to do all in their power to maintain the political momentum in their favour. They did this through the adroit use of propaganda.

Following the suspension of press licensing in 1679, the opposition press met a popular demand for low-cost journalism. Almost 200 pamphlets were published in the period 1679–81 with titles like *The Character of a Popish Successor*, *Reasons for his Majesty's Passing the Bill of Exclusion* and *A Just and Modest Vindication of the Proceedings of the Last Two Parliaments*. Characteristics of the Exclusionist publications included personal attacks on James, dire predictions of the social and economic consequences of the reintroduction of popery, with lurid depictions of popish atrocities, historical arguments justifying Exclusion and denials that the Exclusionists were rebels.

As well as sermons – including some by Oates – and ballads, the opposition publicity machine also made effective use of cartoons, including playing cards with political messages on their reverse such as 'a History of all the Popish Plots that have been in England'. A typical cartoon, *A Prospect of a Popish Successor*, demonized York and portrayed the pope treading the Bible underfoot while a Jesuit held a rosary garlanded with a musket – 'A Right Roman Crucifix'.

Theatre and public ritual were also used to spread the opposition's views. In the play *The Coronation of Queen Elizabeth* the pope got a nun pregnant. The huge November processions held in London in November to celebrate anti-popery were captured in printed and pictorial form for a national readership. The parades would lead off with a bellman solemnly intoning 'Remember Justice Godfrey', followed by a realistic effigy of Godfrey's murdered corpse.

Other forms of political theatricality included the monster

petitions that the Exclusionist leaders got up, complete with tables, pens and ink in the London streets, to agitate for parliament to be allowed to sit during the long prorogation between 1679 and 1680. The anti-Catholic penal laws, dating back to the reign of Elizabeth and imposing ferocious capital punishments on priests and on the lay people who assisted them, were strongly enforced during the period of the Popish Plot and Exclusion and, with their solemn trials and gory executions, helped keep the political temperature at boiling point.

Fourteen Jesuits and a further twenty-one Catholics were put to death throughout the period of Plot and Exclusion; executions in provincial centres spread the propaganda of anti-popery around the country.

Oates, as the initiator of the allegations launched in 1678 retained a central role, but his fame and fortune, including a generous state pension as his reward for alerting the nation to its peril, encouraged other witnesses such as Bedloe and Dugdale to come forward. Oates's charge that the queen was implicated in an attempt to assassinate Charles led to the prosecution of Catherine's physician, Wakeman, along with various Benedictine monks, one of whom was accused of putting up £6,000 to murder the king. A hamfisted effort, the so-called 'Meal Tub Plot', to implicate opposition elements in a plot of their own, backfired. The trial of the Catholic Viscount Stafford, accused by Dugdale of offering £500 for the King's assassination, was accompanied by the full panoply of a legal action in the House of Lords, and his execution, like that of the Irish Catholic prelate Oliver Plunkett and other Irishmen in May 1681, helped feed the atmosphere of conspiracy, alarm and drama. In June 1680 came the audacious attempted prosecutions of York as an ordinary 'popish recusant' and the king's mistress, the Duchess of Portsmouth, as a common prostitute.

Such an atmosphere, of trials for blood and constant revelations and sensations, would seem to suggest conditions of extreme disorder in England in 1679–81. There were, it is true, some signs of instability. The campaign to 'petition' Charles II into granting a sitting of the second Exclusion parliament crystallized the Exclusionist opposition into a political party. The new grouping, underpinned by nearly thirty political clubs in London, including the famous 'Green Ribbon Club', was given the name 'Whigs'. Such party formation in itself seemed to present a problem of political order in a value system that equated partisanship with faction and disruption.

We should not, though, exaggerate the degree of turbulence in England in 1678–81. As the historian J. H. Plumb (1967) has shown, the long-term trend in English political life in the later-seventeenth and early-eighteenth centuries was towards political and social stability. The Exclusion crisis did not significantly interrupt that development. Indeed, the campaign against James's succession might be seen as evidence for the quest for stability – an attempt to avert the predicted chaos that would descend with a popish successor. Led by wealthy peers like Shaftesbury, the Whigs, apart from a republican fringe, upheld monarchy, and their methods were the constitutional ones of trying to obtain the royal assent to parliamentary bills. Their techniques, including the petitioning campaign and the pope-burning processions, were non-violent and orderly.

There was much talk in 1678–81 that '1641' – the year that made civil war inevitable – was come again and that the country was on a downhill course for internecine violence. It is true that one or two individuals, including an MP who was prepared for civil war 'if there be no other way to prevent Popery', were ready for the prospect. However, the very fear of civil war in the period 1679–81 made the return of the conditions of 1641–2 highly unlikely. It is true that many people alive in 1680 – probably the majority – themselves had no direct recollections of the horrors of the 1640s. However, the terrors of civil war had become part of the national culture, talked over in ale-houses, hovels and halls all round the country, handed down in families and dwelt on by journalists and preachers. The latter part of 1679 or the first half of 1680 may have been the crucial period in convincing large numbers of people that the prospect of civil war sparked off by James's exclusion from the succession was a worse outlook than that of a future Catholic succession.

In this period order was kept by the crown's steadily increasing its grip on the country. From 1679, wholesale purges of the county commissions of the peace were putting local government and police into the hands of loyalists. A small standing army existed, the government had recruited able younger ministers such as Lawrence Hyde, Sidney Godolphin and Robert Spencer, Earl of Sunderland and there was peace abroad. In January 1680 Charles felt strong enough to allow James back into England from Scotland, and when the Duke was sent away again in the autumn, it was as the king's official commissioner to govern the northern kingdom.

Undoubtedly, a major contribution to the gradual improvement in the crown's prospects was made by the formation of an anti-Whig loyalist party, the Tories. Just as the campaign to pressure Charles into allowing parliament to sit helped fuse the Exclusionists into the Whig party, so the counter-campaign of 'abhorring' the Whig petitions brought into being a party structure for the expression of loyalism in London and around the country.

All the signs are that a bedrock political loyalism, linked to religious traditionalism, existed in post-Restoration England. As far as most of the nobility, gentry, urban upper-middle class and clergy were concerned, the threat posed in the 1640s and 1650s by militant puritanism to property and social hierarchy cemented their attachment to the Stuart throne and the Church of England as guarantors of the deferential society. We should also be aware, though, of the strength of lower-class royalism. This orientation was consolidated by recollections of the mid-seventeenth-century puritan onslaught on popular culture and recreations and by plebeian bigotry against bourgeois Nonconformists, along with xenophobia aimed against the foreign origins of some Nonconformists. In the course of 1680 and 1681, the possibility of a broad-based Tory coalition in support of the crown against the Whigs and their Nonconformist allies came to be appreciated. James himself noticed the change in 1680:

As for the temper [mood] of the several countries [counties], the judges [touring the realm on their assizes], and all that are come to town do say they find, within these two or three months, the greatest alteration for the better that can be imagined.

The Duke was witnessing here the activation of latent support for monarchist principles around the country. Of course, we must not predate or exaggerate the revival in the crown's fortunes or the swing of opinion in its favour. The attack on James as a recusant in the courts in 1680, though headed off by a resourceful Lord Chief Justice, Scroggs, showed how vulnerable the heir might still be to Shaftesbury's apparently limitless

29

audacity. There was also talk of York's being impeached, and before parliament could reassemble the Duke had been sent away again, to Scotland. This parliament, though, which the king finally allowed to sit in October 1680 when his series of prorogations expired, was to provide a key test for examining the extent of the revival in the crown's fortunes. The parliament was to show that the Tories, though well organized and led, could not yet overturn the effects of Whig militancy in the Commons or head off the increasingly intransigent speeches by Whig hardliners, but that the Lords could and would act as a decisive anti-Whig counterbalance.

The opening moves in the session, including listening to one Dangerfield testify that York had offered him money to concoct a bogus plot and try to foist it on the Whigs, seemed to show how right it had been to send the Duke out of England. The Commons blankly refused to cooperate on foreign policy and taxation, lashed out at 'popishly affected' ministers, began impeachment proceedings against a senior Tory MP and against judges, including Lord Chief Justice Scroggs, made violent attacks on anti-petitioners and set in motion plans for a nation-wide massacre of Catholics. This bloodthirsty mood would certainly have convinced many that a civil war atmosphere was being deliberately stoked up by the Whigs in the Commons. Burnet, a moderate Whig supporter, described the various resolutions as the 'extravagances of resentment and high indignation'. What had occasioned such 'resentment' was the Lords' response to the latest Commons vote for Exclusion. The careful organization of Whig voting in the Commons, their command of procedure and the continuing substantial wavering or un-committed element in the House made it impossible for the Tory group to thwart their will there. A new Exclusion bill had consequently gone through its three readings in the Commons without division. But it had then been thrown out by the Lords, with a division and a vote of sixty three to thirty against. Here is the reason for that bitter 'resentment and high indignation' of the Whigs in the Commons.

The House of Lords was by no means immune to anti-popery and had voted fifty to thirty to convict the Catholic Viscount Stafford. Why, then, did the Lords reject a bill that had passed the Commons, initiated there by the distinguished Lord Russell and 'seconded by several of the most eminent speakers'? The

30

block voting by the bishops against the bill certainly helped defeat it. Several historians have also stressed the importance of the king's prior instructions to the Lords and his presence in the Chamber during the debates and votes, his tall frame with his back to the fire, his dark eyes watching the peers' behaviour. Others, including Burnet, have emphasized the role of George Savile, Earl of Halifax, a former critic of the government but now a court supporter and proponent of limitations. According to Burnet, in successfully arguing against Exclusion, Halifax scored a debating triumph over Shaftesbury – no mean achievement – and the Whigs in the Commons concurred with the view of a one-man victory: 'he had destroyed their bill'.

In reality, though, each of these two interpretations – the effect of the king's presence and the importance of Halifax's achievement in debate – is relatively superficial, and they overlook a slower-working transformation affecting the political nation and much of the nation at large. In particular, what Halifax had to say – that to disinherit the Duke of York would set a bad precedent for all inherited titles to property such as those of their lordships – was very telling. However, the more general perception to which Halifax's comments gave voice – that monarchy in the due line was a guarantee of all property, all hierarchy, all authority, all stability – was a cliché in seventeenth-century political thought.

What the Lords' vote confirmed was that men of property were now in large numbers deeply suspicious of some of the wider implications of Exclusion. Throughout the Exclusion parliaments, there remained a dilemma for many members, torn between what the historian of parliament Hennings calls 'the conflicting pulls of loyalty to the crown and distrust of a Popish heir to the throne'. At the same time, Jones shows that the Whigs' domination of the Commons was becoming less and less a reflection of national trends: 'Although the Exclusion Bill had the unanimous support of the Whigs in the Commons, it was certain to encounter serious opposition in the country as a whole. Negligible and ineffective in the Commons, the Tories formed a considerable section of the nation' (Jones 1970). The time was surely fast approaching for Charles II to test the strength of Tory feeling in the country and to challenge the vociferous and still prevailing commitment to Exclusion of the Commons – a commitment, it has to be said, untested in a

Commons division since May 1679. The embittered second Exclusion parliament was prorogued on 10 January 1681; its dissolution soon afterwards was followed by elections in February and March for a parliament summoned to Oxford for 21 March.

Exclusion at this time was by no means a forlorn hope. In Cheshire, for example, with its Nonconformist traditions and feeling of vulnerability in some districts to neighbouring strongly Catholic parts of Lancashire, twenty-four out of fifty leading landowning families continued to support Exclusion. Whiggery, then, remained the most popular single option, but did not command majority support (in a county with a Whiggish profile) among the sort of families which traditionally supplied a shire's MPs, and was outnumbered by anti-Exclusionists and undecideds. Among the voting freeholders, in areas of the county abutting Lancashire as many as 95 per cent voted for Whig candidates. On the other hand, in the election of the early months of 1681 in Cheshire, the Whig hold was contested for the first time in the Exclusion series, with electoral challenges to Whig incumbents. Seventeen out of the fifty leading families opposed Exclusion and in some divisions of the county Whig candidates polled percentages of the vote as low as 37 or even 13 per cent. That Exclusion was now a cause in retreat rather than advance was even suggested by an ardent supporter of it in the 1680 parliament: '. . . there be eleven to seven now for the interest of a popish successor . . .'.

The king's task was to act decisively, giving a clear lead to shifting opinion. Charles chose to call parliament to Oxford, a decision laden with significance. The move out of London has usually been explained in terms of the king's wish to avoid the capital's heavy (but by no means universal) Whig hegemony, and in particular to escape the menace of Shaftesbury's 'brisk boys', anti-Catholic thugs from the East End. However, Oxford had a powerful symbolic value of its own. Its university was the leading seminary of the Church of England, and Charles was to use his Oxford parliament to announce his realignment with the Established Church as the seal of a new covenant with the Tory party. For another thing, Oxford had been the base of royalism during the civil war, a place of rich associations with Charles I, whose martyr cult was so important an element in Tory image-making.

Dr John Childs (1980) has shown how, in advance of this parliament, Charles used his small but professional army of just over 5,000 to good effect. Units of cavalry were stationed along the London to Oxford road. The king could rely on 660 guards at Oxford itself, and London was put under the command of the Earl of Craven with a large force of nearly 2,000 troopers and orders to crush ruthlessly any signs of disorder. Historians such as J. P. Kenyon have usually emphasized the aggressiveness of the Whigs in the run-up to the Oxford parliament, but it is clear that the military initiative was in fact seized by the king. Indeed, Charles's highly effective use of the troops in March 1681 might suggest that he was at last adopting his brother's militarist proposals. That, though, would give a misleading impression of Charles's essentially political strategy early in 1681. The army movements were back-up precautions to create space for a parliamentary, not a military, outcome. Charles's task now was to present the most attractive possible face of kingship not only by deploying his ingrained courtesy and suppleness as a counter to the bloodthirsty surliness the Whigs had shown in the last parliament, but also by projecting an image of regal firmness. That firmness was on display in the king's speech opening parliament and critically reviewing its recent extremism, 'with some severe reflections on their former proceedings' (Burnet). This was shrewd image-projection; the 'royal politican', as J. R. Jones (1987) calls him, was here addressing a national audience as well as parliament itself. This kingly sternness, though, prefaced an offer of unprecedented conciliation: the scheme of limitations was to be extended into arrangements for a regency in the hands of William and Mary following Charles's death. Charles II was a race-goer and a gambler, and this was his most daring gamble, for the 'Orange option' was an attractive one to the considerable number of people who favoured William and Mary in any case, as well as to those who saw in the idea a formula for the preservation of hereditary succession (James would be king, albeit in name only). Had the Whigs taken up this regency plan, Charles would have been put in the highly embarrassing position of betraying James and indeed the whole future of the English monarchy. However, in gambling that the Whigs would spurn his offer, Charles was gambling wisely and in the process confirming the identification of Shaftesbury's Whigs as irreconcilable and radical extremists.

Charles had in fact made a previous decision to dissolve this parliament early on in its life. Crippling disputes between the two Houses, at loggerheads since the October 1680 Lords vote, and the Commons knee-jerk recourse to a new bill of Exclusion gave the king the pretext he needed. In a moment of high drama, vividly recalled by Burnet, Charles, 'coming to the House of Lords, ... put on his robes in haste, and calling up the Commons, he dissolved the Parliament without any previous notice, and departed instantly to Windsor'. The Whigs melted away.

Professor Jones writes that by this sensational coup Charles put 'an end to Exclusion and effectively to the first Whigs also'. That is largely true, except that the Oxford triumph had to be followed up. It had also had to be carefully prepared for, especially on the financial side. During the Exclusion crisis, Shaftesbury hoped that eventually sheer fiscal need would force Charles to yield to the Commons over Exclusion. But there was no such financial need. As first commissioner of the Treasury, Lawrence Hyde, Earl of Rochester, had instituted cuts in government expenditure (including interruptions of salaries and pensions), untied the Treasury from privy council control, and somehow prevailed on Charles not to spend the surplus now accruing. Reductions in government debts had cut expenditure on interest payments; administrative reforms in the collections of the customs and excise had brought more of the revenue actually into the Exchequer; a cheap foreign policy had reduced expenses; and the resumption of trade with France had fed the customs receipts. Rochester was able to tell the king, from his intimate knowledge of the accounts, that he was now able to live without a parliament.

Much used to be made of the financial value to Charles of a secret deal he did with Louis XIV. By its terms Charles, in return for his neutrality in Europe, was to receive an allowance of three million *livres* spread over three years. However, the financial advantages to Charles of this contract should not be exaggerated. Not all the cash came in, and its total in any case, when set against the overall revenue, put it in the category of top-up money. However, this agreement set the seal on an inactive and hence cheap foreign policy for the remainder of Charles's reign.

The dismissal of the Oxford parliament marked the decisive up-turn in the fortunes of the crown in the reign of Charles II.

Two particular statements made by the king in this parliament should be regarded as highly significant. One was a remark he made pointing to the bench of bishops when he said 'I have the church and nothing will ever separate us'. This renewed commitment to the Church of England was the primary factor in Charles's secure position for the next four years of his reign. His other statement was a longer one, a declaration from the throne in which the king once more reviewed the recent obduracy of parliaments and assured his subjects of his own wish to govern as a Protestant according to the rule of law. Significantly, it was Archbishop Sancroft of Canterbury who proposed that, to give it maximum national publicity, the declaration be read by all Anglican clerics from their pulpits.

Texts like the declaration show how far the monarchy in England, in order to survive intact, had had to step down from the altar of divine-right kingship into the political arena of propaganda so as to win the king's subjects' hearts and minds. As a propaganda manifesto, the declaration evoked a widespread positive response in the form of loyal addresses from various bodies around the country. This response revealed the strength of the Tory swing around England.

4

The second restoration, 1681–5

Several terms have been used by historians to describe the next phase of English political development, from 1681 to 1685. For the 'Whig' (i.e. liberal, anti-Stuart) school, the period saw a renewed attempt on the part of the Stuart dynasty to subvert England's liberties and parliamentary constitution; it was a 'second Stuart absolutism' (the first being the personal government of Charles I between 1629 and 1640). It is true that there were 'absolutist' features in the period, including an army build-up. However, that term 'absolutist' can be misleading and should be used with caution. There was indeed a 'potential for absolutism' (Miller 1984) in late seventeenth-century English (and Scottish) government; the crown's potential powers were very extensive, and much of this potential was realized in the period 1681–5, as England joined a group of other seventeenth-century European states steadily advancing towards authoritarian government. However, this was not a tyranny, and if it was an absolutism it was a legal absolutism, for the king of England's great powers were exercised according to the forms of law. Only once did Charles II break the law between 1681 and his death in 1685 – in 1684, when he quietly ignored the toothless 1664 Triennial Act requiring a parliament every three years.

The label that probably commands the most widespread support as a descriptive tag for the period is 'Tory Reaction'. The phrase certainly reflects the enormous importance of the

Tories in this period, when local government was largely handed over to them. It also suggests to us that the Tories represented an effective block on royal freedom of action; there were clear limits to what Charles II could and could not do and these were set by the Tories. Top of the list of implicit prohibitions would be any climb-down from Charles's commitment to upholding the Church of England, the Tories' talisman. It is also hard to imagine the king getting much Tory support for an actively and publicly pro-French policy. King Charles enjoyed power, prestige and popularity in his last four years, but this was on the implicit understanding that he respect Tory views and prejudices.

Valuable though it is, however, the term 'Tory Reaction', while it recognizes the fundamental importance of the Tories as both a support of, and a constraint on, royal power, exaggerates the role of the party in politics after 1681, overestimates Charles's own commitment to the party and gives insufficient weight to the real revival in the crown's own fortunes in these years. Thus we shall select for the period the term 'the second Restoration', in order to point up the genuine rebuilding of royal power that took place. The royalist poet John Dryden coined this notion of a Restoration restored:

Once more the Godlike *David* [Charles] was Restor'd,
And willing Nations knew their lawful Lord.

Dyrden's poem from which these lines were taken, the first part of *Absalom and Achitophel*, with its portrayal – based on a biblical story – of a treasonable conspiracy by Monmouth and Shaftesbury against Charles II, made an outstanding contribution to a key element in the royalist recovery, the propaganda battle. In July 1681 Shaftesbury was arrested and put in the Tower to face a charge of high treason. As it happened, Dryden's poem came out, some days before Shaftesbury's trial, in November, and traditionally the appearance of the poem has been explained in terms of trying to influence the jury in the case. That may be so, though the task of persuading a jury empanelled by London's and Middlesex's Whig sheriffs to bring in a conviction against the party's presiding genius was probably beyond even Dryden's gifts. The poem was rather part of a massive drive on the part of the crown and the Tories to win nationwide support, especially from the moderate centre.

Light, equable and urbane in tone, *Absalom and Achitophel* uses laughter as its weapon against the Whigs. Dryden's portrait gallery of their chieftains, disguised as biblical characters, includes his justly famous depiction of the absurd Whig aristocrat, George Villiers, second Duke of Buckingham – 'Zimri':

> Stiff in Opinions, always in the wrong;
> Was every thing by starts, and nothing long:
> But in the course of one revolving Moon,
> Was Chymist, Fidler, States-Man, and Buffoon.

Dryden also reflected growing scepticism about the Popish Plot, the original dynamo of Exclusionism:

> Some Truth there was, but dash'd and brew'd with Lyes;
> To please the Fools, and puzzle all the Wise.

His demolition job on Oates –

> His Memory, miraculously great,
> Could plots, exceeding mans belief, repeat;

– helped prepare the way for the informer's downfall, culminating in his punitive fining and imprisonment following an action for slander brought by the Duke of York in 1684.

Accomplished and effective as Dryden's poem was, it had, and was intended to have, a restricted readership. With its message that high culture was menaced by political disturbance and with its classical and Miltonic models, the poem consciously appealed to an elite audience, educated, like Dryden himself, in classical humanism. What was needed for the mass market was a coarser Tory propaganda, the equivalent of the Whig repertoire of 1679–81.

In the field of Tory propaganda, the demotic equivalent of John Dryden was the coordinator of the press campaign and editor of the Tory paper the *Observator*, Roger L'Estrange. The new Tory offensive aimed to link Whiggery with Protestant Nonconformity and with memories of how the Church of England and the ancient constitution had been destroyed in the 1640s by puritan zealots. Puritan-inspired Nonconformity, it was alleged, actually advanced the cause of popery. The Tories used the full range of media that the Whigs had employed – sermons, plays, bonfires, ballads, poems and playing cards, with a particularly skilful exploitation of cartoons. A classic by

L'Estrange himself, 'The Committee', sub-titled 'Popery in Masquerade', showed a panel of Nonconformists coordinating the destruction of monarchy, property, order and even of sexual morals; they are egged on by the pope. *Ad hominem* attacks on Whig leaders were also to the fore. Shaftesbury, surgically fitted with a silver tap to drain fluid from a stomach ulcer, was portrayed with cruel and merciless mockery:

> . . . His Belly carries still a Tap,
> Through which black Treason all its dregs doth strain
> At once, both Excrement of Guts and Brain.

There was an evident public response to the output of Tory opinion-forming, taking the characteristic shape of addresses on various occasions, beginning with the counter-addresses to Whig petitions in 1680 and extending right through the early 1680s; there was, wrote Burnet dismissively, 'a humour of making addresses to the King'. These addresses, and the Tory opinions they expressed, were by no means confined to the social elite; they originated, as Burnet recalled, in groups including apprentices. In the second city of the kingdom, industrial Norwich, Toryism had a definite popular flavour, shown, for example, in a strongly loyalist address of 1681 signed by the 'Loial Freeman' – Norwich freemen being typically small-scale craftsmen in the textile trades. Toryism in Norwich, as in London, Bristol and elsewhere, also had strong social and economic resonances. The city contained communities of Flemish and French Calvinist refugees and their descendants who gravitated towards Nonconformity and who could be thereby linked to the Whigs. Competition for work in Norwich was fierce and in 1682 there were nativist riots against French Huguenot textile workers. Tory popular politics in the East Anglican capital were thus bolstered by xenophobia and bigotry against Protestant Dissent. In London, too, where French immigration reached a peak in the 1680s, fear of industrial competition further inflamed the political atmosphere. And it is clear that the capital, like Norwich and probably other towns around the country, had a lower-class Tory presence. In 1681 2,000 of the Thames watermen submitted a Tory address to the crown; even Whig propaganda alleged that signatories to another loyal address were typically 'Journeymen, Carmen, Porters, Tapsters . . .'; and the clever L'Estrange contrasted easy-living Whig lordlings with the hard-working and 'well-affected' London dockers.

As we have seen, Tory propaganda took a hostile tone towards the Nonconformists. There was indeed a strong community of interest and personnel between the Whigs and the Dissenters. The Whigs were strongly committed to religious toleration for Protestant dissidents and, during the Exclusion period, in constituencies around the country the Nonconformists were the main champions of the Whig interest. It is true that only a minority of Whig MPs were themselves Dissenters – a maximum of 42 out of the 300 Shaftesbury regarded as supporters in 1679. The Dissenters tended to be voting fodder for the Whigs rather than themselves candidates. However, Whig members certainly favoured the Nonconformists and this support was fully reciprocated. In Coventry, for instance, all the Whig members were openly pro-Dissent and it was reported that one election was carried for the Whigs by the 'Dissenting brethren'. The small Nonconformist element in the House was overwhelmingly for Exclusion in May 1679.

Arguably, the Nonconformists damaged their longer-term interests by pledging themselves so heavily to the Whigs in the late 1670s. Charles II was alienated from Dissent by its Whig political profile of 1679–81, and James, who had taken up the cause of Dissent in the mid-1670s, now reverted to stereotypes about the identification of Nonconformity with republicanism. From 1681 the Dissenters paid a high price for their Whiggery. Fines of nearly £10,000 were imposed on a group of eminent Dissenting ministers. In Norwich the Quakers held their meetings in the city prison where large numbers of them were incarcerated, while in Bristol, where three Dissenting meeting houses were vandalized by the mob, 150 Quakers were in gaol by the middle of 1682. In both London and Bristol numbers of Nonconformists died as a result of imprisonment. In strongly Nonconformist Coventry, in January 1684, upwards of 200 Dissenters were presented at the quarter sessions for not attending church and imprisoned for worshipping at their own 'conventicles'.

The acute sufferings of the Nonconformists stand out all the more clearly when contrasted with the relative mildness shown to the Catholics in the last years of Charles's reign. In various counties convictions for popish recusancy fell off sharply after

1681, and in Middlesex, whereas 70 per cent of those convicted for non-attendance at church in 1679 were identifiable Catholics, after 1681 the proportion fell to 6 per cent. In Norwich, in January 1681, it was reported that 'above 50 protestante decenters were prosecuted upon the Act made against papists'. The recusancy laws passed to enforce church attendance were now, writes John Miller, 'being used mainly against Dissenters' (1987).

Much of the initiative for the campaign against Dissent arose from local power struggles in county, and especially in municipal, government. The Nonconformists were largely urban-based, and during the Whig ascendancy the 1661 Corporations Act, which excluded Nonconformists from the government of the borough, was widely ignored. In Coventry, the persecution of Dissenters in 1684 was aimed against the Tories' political enemies, nineteen Dissenters presented at the sessions being Whig corporation members.

The crown's own interest in urban goverment in the 1680s emerged in the first instance from the perceived problem of London. The great city had over the centuries acquired an array of liberties and chartered privileges of extensive self-government, and to those inclined to an absolutist outlook, London hardly seemed part of the king's dominion at all but a kind of independent republic and free city. The opportunity and the need to take on London first became apparent with the attempted trial of Shaftesbury. The Earl was arrested in July 1681 but saved because the elected Whig sheriffs of London and Middlesex empanelled a Whig jury which returned a verdict that there was no case to answer. However, in 1682 the Tories won the elections for sheriff, giving them access to the selection of juries. The sagacious Shaftesbury saw that the game was up and left the country late in the year, dying in Holland in January 1683.

The immediate judicial problem had thus been solved but up to 1683 there remained the wider issue of London's exact relationship to the king's government. An enquiry into London's charter had commenced late in 1681, following Shaftesbury's acquittal. The specific charges were that the city had exceeded its powers by levying an onerous rate (for urban improvements) on the citizens and that the corporation had encouraged sedition and rebellion by petitioning the king to allow parliament to sit in

1680. During the trial the issue of political ideology – the clash between centralist absolutism and autonomous local government as a defence of the rights of the subject – was made plain, with the Lord Chief Justice arguing that failure to annul London's charter would imply that 'you have set up so many independent commonwealths', while another senior judge added, 'and if the law should be otherwise it would erect as many independent republics in the kingdom as there are corporations'. In 1683 the court ruled 'that the franchises and liberty of London be taken into the King's hands'.

The legal and political collapse of the metropolis gave little hope of successful resistance to central government in other, lesser towns and cities, especially as local Tory groups enthusiastically engineered surrenders of charters of self-government. In Norwich, a Tory majority in the corporation carried the surrender in September 1682, designed as an explicitly Tory gesture 'to avoid the least suspicion of contest with your Crowne Imperiall And to give the utmost demonstration of our Loyalty'. Bristol, faced with a trial of its charter, surrendered in 1683 and got its new charter in 1685: in the now standard form, the crown nominated the new corporation and reserved to itself the right of removal both of key officials and of elected personnel. The nationwide process gathered momentum, with fourteen new charters in 1682–3, rising to 76 during nine months in 1685. To a large extent, English municipal government had been brought within the parameters of Tory absolutism. Local power was handed to the crown's Tory friends.

A further indication of the court's recovery was the return of the Duke of York early in 1682. James and his wife stopped off at Norwich where the rising tide of loyalism was reflected in their welcome 'with great joy . . . by a great number of gentlemen [and they were] splendidly entertained by the mayor and aldermen'. In London, too, mass demonstrations at York's return produced cries of 'No Whig, no Whig' and 'God Bless the King and his Royal Highness; no Bill of Exclusion'.

The recovery in Tory and court fortunes had the effect of driving the Whigs into acts of violence and extremism that further damaged their image. In autumn 1680 Essex had proposed a defensive anti-Catholic 'Association' along the lines of the one formed to defend Queen Elizabeth against Mary Queen of Scots in 1685, and Shaftesbury was put on a committee to draft a document. In Shaftesbury's indictment of 1681 it was testified that a paper of Association was taken from the Earl's closet upon his arrest. The draft outlined the encouragement given to popish plotters by the Duke of York's religion and right of succession, complained of his political prominence and the disruptive activities of his servants and proposed an Association in defence of Protestantism and the king's life, to be directed 'by force of arms if need require' so as to prevent James or any other Catholic from succeeding.

The phrase 'by force of arms' provided a field day for Tory propaganda, for it apparently confirmed the link between Whiggery and civil war. The government *Gazette* ran a feature on 'The Two Associations', printing a Parliamentarian Association of 1643 alongside the Shaftesbury version. Whig attempts to suggest that the document was a forgery were met by a stream of Tory addresses including one from Norwich which alleged that the Association was designed to destroy monarchy by levying war and which stood defiantly by the 'Legall Succession and Grandeur of ye English Monarchy'. A further sign of the times was when a motion to denounce the Association was put to the London Common Council.

The alleged link between Whiggery and extremism seemed confirmed by the increasing openness of Monmouth's bid for the throne; his support by popular forces made this all the more abhorrent to the majority of the ruling class. In September 1682 Monmouth began a tour of parts of the Midlands and the north-west, where he was acclaimed, it was reported, by the 'rabble' and 'the vulgar sort of people'. The threat of force during this 'progress', popular rioting in Chester against the gentry and the Cathedral and Monmouth's now unmistakable bid for the succession seemed to complete the identification of his cause with violence and democracy. On 20 September, at the king's command, the Duke was arrested.

Monmouth's arrest drove some Whigs into even more desperate ventures which strengthened the swing of opinion against them. Deprived of a parliamentary forum, Whig groups sought increasingly drastic solutions in 1683. In March of that year a fire destroyed much of the king's holiday town of Newmarket. In consequence, Charles and James left the town earlier than they had planned and thereby, it was later revealed, thwarted a plan by a group of republicans, old Cromwellian troopers and radical Dissenters to assassinate the royal duo as they passed by a property on the London–Newmarket road called the Rye House.

The 'Rye House Plot', as it was immediately named, scared Charles II in ways that the fabricated Popish Plot had not. Testimony by an informant, Robert West, was joined by that of an apostate Whig, Lord Howard of Escrick. In the round-up of suspects that followed the disclosure of the Rye House Plot, leading Whigs met their ends. They included the king's former minister and convinced Exclusionist, the Earl of Essex, who committed suicide in the Tower, Algernon Sidney, son of the Earl of Leicester and author of an anti-absolutist draft treatise, *Discourse concerning Government*, and Lord William Russell, heir to the mighty earldom of Bedford. Thus an important aspect of the reaction following the Rye House Plot was the way the crown was able to subdue some of the great baronial families which might have provided some focus of opposition to an increasing royal absolutism. At the same time, Monmouth's cause seemed destroyed with his flight to Holland in 1684.

The increased confidence of the court allowed for James's readmission to favour – to the cabinet council and, in all but name, to his admiralty command. The open violence of the Rye House Plot further polarized the country by seemingly identifying Whigs and Dissenters as bloodthirsty revolutionaries. An air of aggressive Tory triumphalism is reflected in the flood of addresses congratulating Charles and James on their escape by means of miraculous divine aid, confirming the image of a monarchy and dynasty under God's special protection. The addresses from the Lancashire parliamentary boroughs of Liverpool and Wigan fully caught the mood. Liverpool corporation denounced the 'factious and restless sort of men who cannot endure prerogative, because it secures the property of your Maties good subjects, over whom, they would tyrannize as formerly they have done' [in the Interregnum]. The borough of Wigan concentrated its ire on the alleged link between Whig radicals, republicans and Nonconformists: 'Factious Republicans and Fanatick Zealots . . . Fanatick Sectaries and Seditious Conventiclers'. The use of such language, like the new offensive launched against Nonconformists, indicates the intensification of Tory partisanship in the country.

The same is true of a ringing statement put out by the

University of Oxford in the wake of the Plot. In defence of the king from 'the machinations of traitorous heretics and schismatics', the University Convocation rounded on political doctrines such as 'All civil authority is derived originally from the people', or 'King Charles the First was lawfully put to death'; the 'badge' of the Church of England, the University concluded, was the belief that 'submission and obedience' to the king were to be 'clear, absolute, and without exception'. Events a few years later in the same decade would, as we shall see, severely test the University's and the Church of England's adherence to such beliefs.

The Rye House Plot should be seen as the last splutter from a period of intense national excitement and involvement that had begun with another plot five years before. In the sunset of Charles II's reign – 'good King Charles's golden years' – trade continued to pick up, there was peace at home and abroad and taxes were both low and legal. The centre of political gravity between the Rye House Plot and the end of the reign shifted back to the court. At court the main factors were: the increasing strength of James and his allies as a 'reversionary interest' in which people began to invest their futures; Charles's continuing quest for ministerial balance, or rather for ruling by dividing; and the continuing self-assertion of the crown – as demonstrated in the release of the Catholic peers and of the Earl of Danby.

It is a fascinating exercise to speculate on how Charles's reign might have developed had he not died when he did. Would absolutism have been consolidated or would Charles have shifted to more conciliatory policies, including a reconciliation with Monmouth? We shall never know, for Charles, to all appearances in the peak of middle-aged good health, succumbed to a stroke and died, a deathbed convert to Rome, in February 1685. His departure gave full scope to the sententious moralizing of the obituarists, full of grave reflections on the man of parts flawed by sensuality, and so forth. For all that, Charles II had left an impressive political inheritance behind him and the balance sheet of his achievements allows us also to assess the strength of the crown in 1685 and the real extent of the trend towards absolutism in England by that time. During the Exclusion crisis the king and his allies had fought off a major constitutional challenge from the House of Commons and had successfully asserted key prerogative powers such as those of prorogation and dissolution. The concept of the succession in the due line of descent – one vital to the maintenance of monarchy by divine right – had been vindicated over the elective principle embedded in the campaign for the exclusion of the Duke of York. Charles had re-established a political leadership of the Church of England that belonged to him constitutionally as its supreme governor. The control of local government from the centre had been expanded as never before and the court's enemies had been purged from positions of power. The Whigs were crushed in 1681 and lost the first generation of their leaders in 1683. The crown's finances were relatively healthy (see above, p. 34) and England, if not a mighty force in Europe, was not involved in war or dangerous alliances. Charles left an army of nearly 10,000 men in infantry and cavalry regiments in England, alongside other companies, and troops in Scotland, Ireland and elsewhere. The king had been spending about £200,000 p.a. on building up this professional army – an indispensable prerequisite of absolutism – and his successor was to continue developing it. All in all, James II inherited an enviable legacy of royal power from his brother.

5

'A man for arbitrary power'?:
James II, 1685–7

Considering the furore over the succession in the period 1679–81, the ease with which James II entered into his inheritance in February 1685 is remarkable. Evidence from the capital and from around Britain strongly suggests an overwhelming acclamation of the new accession. A great many of James's subjects seemed to be prepared to accept him in the public capacity of a king and the private capacity of a Catholic. He himself was firm, business-like and kingly, and his application and high seriousness put him a favourable position to exercise his extensive powers.

In what ways was James likely to use these powers? In his accession address to the privy council he was reassuring: he would rule in as moderate and consensual a fashion as could be desired, patterning himself on Charles's 'great clemency and tenderness to his people'. He had been depicted, he said, as 'a man for arbitrary power', but in fact he aimed to rule the nation 'in all its just rights and liberties'; and he made an explicit commitment to uphold the Church of England as a church of 'good and loyal subjects'. It was the best possible beginning.

A small cloud on the horizon concerned the king's revenues, a key part of which, the customs and excise, had been granted to Charles II for life but not to the crown beyond that point. Collecting revenue without a parliamentary grant might have put a question-mark over James's reassurances about governing

47

constitutionally. However, advice from the judges, together with the prevailing inclination to accommodate the king's needs and wishes, allowed the monies in question to be collected pending a parliament. Meanwhile, the disposal of senior government positions gave grounds for further encouragement about the king's moderation. Halifax, the essential centrist, who had earned James's gratitude by his opposition to Exclusion, was retained as Lord President, while Lawrence Hyde, now Earl of Rochester, James's staunchly Anglican brother-in-law, had the high office of Lord Treasurer revived for him. The presence in the government of the former Exclusionists Godolphin and Sunderland seemed to show that James bore no grudges. Certainly no Catholic 'kitchen cabinet' emerged. As far as religion itself was concerned, the new king publicly ignored the Anglican services in the chapel royal and built a fine Catholic chapel, but he did not force attendance on his Protestant ministers or courtiers.

Harmony characterized the preparations and elections for the parliament required at the beginning of the new reign. Commentators such as Burnet emphasized – perhaps over-emphasized – the court manipulation that went into winning these contests: 'much art [was] used to manage elections so as to procure one [a parliament] that would please the king'. There is, indeed, considerable evidence of assiduous management. In York, the Tory Sir John Reresby 'found I was to use all diligence and spare no charge, if I expected success'. Reresby canvassed from door to door and spent an astronomical £350 on drink to buy votes. In Norfolk and Surrey, the Duke of Norfolk leaned on the Justices of the Peace and Deputy Lieutenants of the militia to produce a unanimous choice of 'fit', that is, loyalist, candidates. In Lancashire, the Earl of Derby ordered the militia into the county town to prevent an anti-Tory riot on the part of the 'rabble', while every effort was made to thwart the candidacy of the Monmouth Whig, Lord Brandon. Like the Duke of Norfolk, the Earl also worked to unite gentry 'interests' so that agreed Tory candidates would be returned virtually unopposed. Similar pressures were exerted by other influential figures in other areas. It was also the case that the recall and reissue of borough charters since 1681 had the effect of installing Tory slates of aldermen and councillors in town halls; this too had a striking electoral impact.

To assume, however, that the elections of 1685 were won for

the court through manipulation rather than for the Tories through a continuing swing of opinion overlooks the independence from king and court that this overwhelmingly Tory parliament was to show once it had sat. Initially, it is true, the Commons revealed a highly deferential attitude to the crown, failing to challenge the collection of the customs and excise and abandoning a demand that all religious dissidents, including Catholics, be prosecuted. However, it was on the religious issue, and specifically on that of Catholics in the armed forces, that this parliament was to show itself one made up of independent-minded Tory Anglicans rather than of court lackeys. Independence of mind came all the more easily since the members were also men of landed wealth: 'such a landed Parliament was never seen', commented the Tory Earl of Ailesbury.

As a general assembly of the Anglican and landed interest, the new parliament confronted a crisis that at first deepened the solidarity between it and the king. Radical Whiggery continued to have an appeal amongst elements of the 'middling sort' in the population. Typically, these were small farmers and craftsmen, often struggling, frequently Nonconformist in orientation, violently anti-Catholic, not least because of the associations of popery with royal absolutism, and with a republican, 'levelling', egalitarian and democratic streak to their politics. A rising at the beginning of the reign that comprised the above elements had the effect of strengthening the alliance between the monarchy and the Anglican and propertied ruling class. In June 1685, striking at what he hoped would be a weak point near the transition between two reigns, Monmouth appeared in the West Country to throw down his challenge to James's rule as the champion of Protestant plebeians.

Did Monmouth have any realistic chance of succeeding? His rebellion was coordinated in the sense that it was part of a two-pronged offensive, aiming to confuse the government's reaction. While Monmouth himself raised the Protestant south-west, the powerful Scottish clan chieftain, Argyll, was to exploit religious dissent in south-west Scotland. These two wings of the movement were in fact conceived as parts of a much wider insurrection in which areas where Monmouth was thought to have support, such as London and Cheshire, would rise up in a coordinated campaign. Despite these strategic hopes, the timing of the bid was poor, if only because new governments tend to have a honeymoon relationship with those they govern. In particular, James II had not yet begun the headlong promotion of Catholics that was to alienate so much of the nation by 1688. Had Monmouth stayed his hand, had he lived and made his move three years later, there is no knowing what he might have achieved. As we shall see, an invasion in 1688 in opposition to James did succeed in toppling him from his throne. But in 1685, unlike 1688, the king acted resolutely in his own defence and, no less important, the ruling class, with equal determination, came to his aid.

The attitude of most men of wealth and power to Monmouth's attempted coup is well captured by John Evelyn:

> Such an inundation of phanaticks and men of impious principle must needs have caus'd universal disorder, cruelty, injustice, rapine, sacrilege, and confusion, an unavoidable civil war and misery without end.

This kind of reaction was, if anything, intensified by the radical Whig manifesto issued on Momouth's behalf and including demands for annual parliaments and a repeal of all the laws against Nonconformity. Apparently, a decision had been made to appeal to particular social strata – the popular classes with the Dissenters – at the expense of conservatives and Anglicans whose support for the crown, if ever in doubt beforehand, was now solidly consolidated. In the West Country itself, Burnet reported, 'few of the gentry came into' the Duke's camp.

Monmouth himself, after delaying at Lyme Regis, slowly advanced on the Somerset textile centre and county town, Taunton. Following his bold announcement of his kingship on 20 June, he left Taunton (to be retaken by the royal army) and moved up the central West Country by way of the Somerset towns of Bridgewater, Wells and Shepton Mallet. From the point of view both of morale and the strategic future of his campaign, the Duke now needed to take Bristol, giving him the key to the Severn Valley. Bristol's capture would present Monmouth with tantalizing alternative strategic plans – either a quick dash along the short, straight line from Bristol to London or a long march along the Welsh border, rounding up his supporters in the West Midlands and Cheshire prior to a final assault on the capital. But Bristol was denied the Protestant Duke through the prompt actions of the Dukes of Somerset and

Beaufort, Lords Lieutenant respectively of Somerset and Gloucestershire. Monmouth's cause was effectively crushed late in June by that failure to take the western metropolis.

Falling back on Bridgewater pursued by the king's commander, Feversham, Monmouth decided on a desperate last confrontation with the royal forces at Sedgemoor, just outside the north Somerset town on 6 July; but an attack, in which the Duke's amateur host had the initial advantage of surprise, turned into a rout and then a massacre. Large numbers of Monmouth's West-Countrymen stood their ground to the end, facing the standing army's raking fire 'until the soldiers were weary of killing'. Around 1,500 rebels fell in the Battle of Sedgemoor. Momouth himself, found in a ditch in an unconvincing disguise, appealed cravenly to James for his life but was promptly and barbarically executed in July.

The sequel to the Monmouth uprising comprised a judicial and punitive process and a military rethink. As part of the judicial process, one hundred insurgents were hanged under martial law in the immediate sequel to Sedgemoor and a further 300 were sentenced to hanging, drawing and quartering in George Jeffreys' 'Bloody Assize', a special court of judicial terror. In addition, 1,000 were sent, to the profit of courtiers, as indentured servants to the West Indies.

The numbers selected for capital punishment – roughly equivalent to the 450 peasants executed for their part in the Revolt of 1569 against Queen Elizabeth – suggest the traditional government policy of teaching the lower orders in a given region a post-revolt punitive lesson of deterrence. Further, the fact that noble and officer-corps participants were reprieved confirms the impression that the mass killings were designed to protect the regime in future by reinstilling the lesson that the lower classes had a duty only to obey, never to rebel. Traditionally, the use of judicial savagery against rebels from the lower orders through the use of harsh public executions was deliberately designed to deter through intimidation, based on an acute perception of the state's military weakness in the face of peasant revolt.

Yet any such motive of deterrence in the Bloody Assize was now rapidly becoming outmoded. Thanks to decades of improvement in cavalry, gunnery and tactics and to the more recent build-up of a paid force, the time was fading fast when, by sheer weight of numbers, a plebeian host could in any effective way challenge the state. Feversham's explanation of his somewhat relaxed movements in the West in terms of his wish to avoid slaughter of the insurgents was in fact borne out by the ease with which his regulars, though outnumbered by 5–6,000 to 2,000, saw off the rebel volunteers at Sedgemoor. In other words, even in terms of state security, there was no need for the cruelty of the Bloody Assize. James's government, when backed by the bayonets of his professional army, could never be seriously threatened by the kind of traditional peasant-and-worker revolt that Monmouth tried to lead.

That is not to say that there was no need for a review of the military conduct of the campaign, which showed up areas of concern over the behaviour of the militia, an amateur force whose military prowess left much to be desired. One possible conclusion to be drawn from the military post-mortem was that the army's professionalism needed to be enhanced: the king should be served by the best troops available – regardless, James himself would have argued, of inconvenient and irrelevant religious disqualifications.

During the emergency, James had infiltrated about a hundred Roman Catholics into an army that was rapidly approaching 20,000 in number. As well as aiming to attract able officers, the king was also planning to use the army as a vehicle through which to remove legal discrimination against Catholics, thereby hoping to encourage conversions. When parliament returned after its recess during the rebellion, this question of the Catholic officers strained relations between the king and the Commons, an early warning of a later estrangement. Underlying the House's fears was the traumatic prospect of a royal praetorian guard, made up of men of alien religion and even race and divorced by their popery from English political culture. James's parliament of loyalists was indeed willing to seek agreement with the king. However, the 1673 Test Act, they insisted, was still the law of the land. Seemingly unaware of the depth of feeling in the House, the king, in a speech of 9 November, invited the members to ignore the problem:

Let no man take exception that there are some officers in the army not qualified, according to the late Tests, for their employments. The gentlemen . . . are most of them well known to me, and . . . I think fit now to be employed under me.

The House countered on 16 November with an address combining, as they said, 'great deference and duty' with unmistakable defiance:

> those officers cannot by law be capable of their employments, and . . . the incapacities they bring upon themselves thereby can no ways be taken off but by an Act of Parliament.

Thus before James's first year was out, he had come to an impasse with the most loyal parliament that ever a Stuart monarch met. On 20 November 1685 he prorogued parliament until the following February, but it was in fact never to meet again during his reign. Evidently buoyed up now by the crushing of the Monmouth revolt, with a sense as he said, of 'a more than ordinary providence', reserving him for some great task, James resolved to advance the cause of Catholicism by advancing individual Catholics. To get his way over the Catholic officers, the king would turn next to the courts of law. There in 1686 James determined to test the validity of his claim to exempt persons from the operation of certain laws: the 'dispensing power'.

Many believed that such a discretionary power was a necessary component of monarchical sovereignty, giving rulers the ability to cut through the Gordian knots of the law's delays. One of the Catholic officers, Sir Edward Hales, was prosecuted for serving in the army in defiance of the 1673 Test Act. Hales pleaded the king's dispensation and the case went to Lord Chief Justice Herbert, who consulted the senior judiciary (which had already been pressurized and weeded by James) for a verdict.

In his summation delivering the judgment of eleven out of twelve of the leading judges, Herbert rightly described the case as one 'of great consequence' and went on to make extreme claims for the crown's power to stultify statute law and in effect to legislate without parliament: 'There is no law whatsoever but may be dispensed with by the supreme lawgiver [the king] . . . the laws of England are the king's laws.'

This decision setting the king above the law opened the way for a wholesale Catholicization of the armed forces and civil service. As we shall see, James also had his eye on opportunities for his fellow-Catholics in academia, controlled though this was by the Church of England, under the provisions of the 1662 Act of Uniformity. Was James, then, pursuing aggressive policies towards the Church of England from 1686 onwards? Professor Kenyon (1966) emphasizes rather James's nervy defensiveness towards his subjects. According to this analysis, the king, in appointing co-religionst allies to key civilian and military offices, was simply seeking to restore in his own favour the precarious balance of forces in the realm and to defend his position from attack. To find the exact balance between aggression and defence in James's conduct *vis-à-vis* the Church and the Anglican establishment, it is necessary to examine his ecclesiastical campaign of 1686–7.

In the first place, with royal encouragement, including cash subsidies, Catholic conversionary tactics were being assiduously pursued, especially by means of the press, where, for example, the sermons delivered in the royal chapel were published. John Evelyn noticed the assertiveness of the Catholic revival from the very beginning of the reign, with 'Popish pamphlets and pictures sold publickly . . .'. The Church, on the other hand, in a royal order of March 1686, *Directions Concerning Preaching*, was deprived of any right to rely: Anglican homilies were to contain no adversarial theology – no 'abstruse and speculative notions' – but were to restrict themselves in effect to moral precepts. The ban, in an age passionately devoted to confrontational theologizing, left the established Church with its hands tied behind its back. One leading churchman, John Sharp, rector of St-Giles-in-the-Fields, London, defied this ban by purporting to give pastoral advice to parishioners on withstanding the blandishments of popery. When James ordered Bishop Henry Compton of London to silence Sharp, Compton counselled rather than disciplined him. Compton, the proudly aristocratic brother of the Earl of Northampton, was the stoutest champion of pure Protestantism on the bench of bishops. He had earlier been dismissed from the privy council, and now his refusal to take effective action against Sharp invited royal disciplinary action against him, in what was to be the most serious clash between Church and state in England for over a century. Having taken action to suppress anti-Catholic preaching in York as well as London, by the summer of 1686 the king could be seen as defending the Church of Rome by conducting a campaign of aggression against the Church of England.

Yet James was still supreme governor of that Church, with powers over it that needed to be exercised. Perhaps some form of ecclesiastical commission was called for to execute the king's governorship in its more practical details. There were certainly good precedents for such a commission, including, as recently as the period 1681–4, a panel to implement the monarch's powers of appointment, the Commission for Ecclesiastical Promotions, which had been a potent weapon for consolidating a firm Tory presence in the clergy. Yet in setting up commissioners to superintend the Church – the Commissioners for Ecclesiastical Causes – in July 1686, James was certainly not surrendering any royal powers over the established Church. This was a body in which the king's control over the Church was in fact reaffirmed, albeit with a view to undermining the Church's position. The Commission was dominated by some of James's most loyal servants, Sunderland – now moving towards Catholicism – and the absolutist lawyers Jeffreys and Herbert. The most significant decision of the Commission was the suspension of Compton in September.

Apart from the suspension of Compton, a foremost task of the Commission was to aid the king in the creation of a Catholic interest in the universities. This campaign operated on the basis of two main considerations. First, the universities affected the upbringing of the ruling class, and Catholic tutors could play a vital role in obtaining conversions. Second, university posts were prestigious and in some cases, as at Magdalen College, Oxford, generously rewarded. James's attempts to intrude Catholics into Oxford and Cambridge should be seen in terms of his intention to introduce reverse discrimination in favour of his fellow Catholics and to remove the career drawbacks of their faith. The king's 'university policy', begun in 1686, continued into the next year and helped confirm his estrangement from the Church of England.

The king's campaign targeted both universities. He began by trying – unsuccessfully – to get Cambridge to confer a degree on a Benedictine monk and then successfully imposed a Catholic master on Sidney Sussex College. Meanwhile in Oxford, at University College, the master, Obadiah Walker, was already in place when he announced his conversion to Catholicism and was allowed to stay put. At Christ Church, Oxford, James appointed a junior fellow, John Massey, a Catholic or Catholic sympathizer, as master and went on to intrude a Romanist wedge at Magdalen College, Oxford, by installing a Catholic fellow in what Burnet said was 'esteemed the richest foundation in England, perhaps in Europe'. But here the king was checked.

The contest over Magdalen was bitter and protracted. Following the death of the president of the college towards the end of March 1687, James ordered the fellows to elect as his successor Anthony Farmer, a man who was disqualified on every imaginable count, not least for his notorious morals. (He even arranged a strip-show for the undergraduates.) It was only Farmer's Catholicism, or at least his non-Anglicanism, that could possibly recommend him to the king, and the fellows felt they were on good ground in standing by their college statutes, defying the royal mandamus (letter of installation of a nominee) and going ahead with the election of one of their own number, the upright Anglican Dr Hough. In the months of confused wrangling that followed, James alienated the university that had resoundingly declared its belief in non-resistance to kings but four years before. In the stormiest scene of his reign, James, during a personal visit to Oxford in September 1687, tried to bully the fellows into submission, but in truth he was mismanaging the whole business and could not even carry the whole of the Ecclesiastical Commission with him. Until he had the recalcitrant fellows dismissed – when he almost certainly exceeded his legal powers – James had not acted unconstitutionally towards Magdalen. But he *had* behaved crassly, trying to foist a worthless leader on a proud institution of learning. Once again, James's political judgment had been exposed as seriously defective. He had managed to alienate those 'old friends' of monarchy, the men of the Church of England, and words he uttered at Oxford indicate that he was aware of the breach: he had, he said, 'no enemy but among those who call themselves Church of England men'.

6

The search for new allies: James II, 1687–8

James had by now forfeited much of the good will of the Tory and Church interest. Could he find new friends and allies? His fellow Catholics, on whose behalf he laboured, were – or were thought to be – a phalanx of support. However, they were few in number, spread out in the more distant regions, politically inexperienced and educationally deprived. In addition, some aristocratic Catholics expressed misgivings about the dangerous consequences for Catholics themselves of James's more radical measures such as the promotion of Catholic officers. However, if Catholic support was weak, James believed he could forge an alliance with another group of men and women penalized simply for not being members of the Church of England: the Protestant Dissenters.

What was James's attitude to the Nonconformists and to the wider but related issue of religious toleration? The evidence seems conflicting, because James's views on this question were partly coloured by changing political circumstances. As long before as 1669, it had been reported of him that he lacked 'bitterness against the nonconformists, he was against all persecution merely for conscience's sake, looking upon it as an unchristian thing and absolutely against his conscience . . .'. Committed, then, as he may have been to religious toleration in theory – and from 1673 seeing himself as a victim of religious intolerance – in practical and political terms James was suspicious of the Dissenters' alleged links with republicanism, of their proven alliance with the Whigs during the Exclusion campaign and of the support of some of them for Monmouth in 1685. At his accession he had given the clergy of the Church of England a guarantee that he would uphold the laws protecting the Church; as he told a bishop in 1685, 'he would never give any sort of countenance to dissenters'. In the year of his accession, the king's attitude to religious dissidence and to the wider issue of toleration was tested by Louis XIV's revocation of the Edict of Nantes – that is to say, of the royal decree which had granted the Protestants in France the right to exist. A historian who has made a study of this question speculates that, though James did not support persecution, he approved of the revocation, regarding the French Protestants as republicans.

James, then, may well have been drawn to religious toleration in principle, but his actual view of dissident Protestants was largely dictated by political considerations and images. His need for political allies following the refusal of the Anglicans to support him in advancing Catholicism in 1686–7 persuaded him of the necessity of an understanding with the Nonconformists who, as the French ambassador reported, were to be 'allied to the Catholics in such a way that together they might form a party against the episcopalian [Anglican] element . . . which had opposed and reduced the efficacy of the measures so far taken in favour of the Catholic faith'. James's appreciation of the need for allies against the anti-Catholic Anglican majority induced him to adopt tolerant policies towards Dissenting groups, to change his political perceptions of Dissenters and to accept more unequivocally the principles of religious toleration in themselves. As early as 1686, the Quakers, widely regarded since their origins in the 1650s as the most intransigent of Dissenters but in fact by now overwhelmingly pacifists who abjured radical political activism, were let off the penalties for absence from parish worship; and a persecuting magistrate was told that the king did not wish 'to have these people so troubled upon the account of their being Quakers only'.

James's view of Quakers in particular and, by extension, of Dissenters at large was partly shaped by personal relations and by economic considerations. It is characteristic of the way James viewed the world in terms of personal loyalties and relationships that his attitude to the Quakers was influenced by his cordial understanding with such leading Quakers as the theologian Robert Barclay and the political organizer and colonial developer William Penn. Penn himself reported James to have told him that 'he looked upon us as a quiet and industrious people'. Therein lies the clue to James's favourable perception of the Nonconformists from an economic perspective. Concerned as Duke of York with trading and colonial development, James as king was committed to fostering a national commercial progress in which the thrifty, enterprising and diligent Dissenters might play a key part: hence his moves to encourage the immigration of foreign skilled workers. Indeed, Professor Miller sees James's abandonment of the Anglicans and his adoption of the Nonconformists as accompanying a shift in crown economic and fiscal policy away from favouring the land, the gentry and agriculture and in favour of the middling classes, the towns, trade and money. Holland provided the outstanding example of a prosperous commercial society that had thriven through state-guaranteed religious pluralism. As royal electoral agents were told in 1687–8 during the preparation for a new parliament intended to repeal the Test Acts, 'You are . . . to inform those you converse with that liberty of conscience hath been the cause of the Hollanders' great trade, riches and power.'

There were clear limits to James's benevolence to the Dissenters. He showed no signs of wishing to throw open the doors of the universities to the Nonconformists, as Penn wanted. Nor did he promote them in the armed forces. Nevertheless, he was by 1687 genuinely convinced of the value of religious toleration, and his new covenant with the Nonconformists was set out in the first of his two Declarations of Indulgence, in April 1687. The king had tried the unsuccessful method of 'closetting' – bringing heavy pressure to bear on MPs to get them to support parliamentary repeal of the Test Acts, which he regarded as the greatest single barrier to his plans for the advancement of Catholics. He now dreamed of a Dissenter-dominated House of Commons which would accede to repeal once he had won the Nonconformists' favour by offering them toleration.

In his Declaration of Indulgence of April 1687, James spoke of his wish to unite all his subjects around the twin pillars of property and religious freedom. In a remarkably frank admission, he said he wished all his subjects were Catholics but insisted that conscience should not be constrained. High on the list of arguments he presented in favour of toleration was the view that intolerance, 'by spoiling trade, depopulating countries and discouraging strangers' [immigrants], was against the interests of the state. James also maintained that, ever since the reign of Elizabeth, persecution had failed in its aim of securing total adhesion to the Church. He expected, he said, eventual parliamentary agreement to toleration, and he restated his commitment to the protection and maintenance of the Church of England.

In a sweeping programme of toleration, James suspended all ecclesiastical penalties for non-attendance at church and for not receiving the Anglican holy communion. Further, he gave all his subjects freedom of religious assembly. The Declaration went much further than the later 1689 Toleration Act in that it exempted no denomination from its benefits and specified no theological preconditions for tolerance. The authorities were to protect religious services from attacks. There was to be no religious testing for office under the crown.

James's Declaration of Indulgence was in every respect a remarkable document, anticipating as it did by much more than a century the arrival of full civil rights for religious minorities in Britain. What were the reactions to this measure and in particular what were the reactions of the Dissenters, the vital element in James's equation? The Nonconformists were divided in their response, largely along denominational lines. Among the Presbyterians, the denomination closest to the Church of England, there was a tendency to be suspicious. The Presbyterian leader Daniel Williams even said he would prefer to continue being persecuted rather than accept an unconstitutional toleration, while Richard Baxter confessed his reluctance to alienate 'the body of conforming clergy' by accepting the Indulgence. On the other hand, the openly secessionist sects, particularly the Quakers, welcomed the relief measure. In 1687, 1,660 Quakers were let out of prison and William Penn led a delegation to the king from the Quakers' London Yearly Meeting in grateful support. Nonconformist congregations generally tended to pressurize their pastors to respond positively, and eighty addresses of thanks were presented by congregations and ministers around the country. When James visited Coventry, with its large Dissenter community, in September 1687, he was greeted gratefully by 'about two hundred citizens (most of them Dissenters)

. . . to whom the King behaved with much respect'. On the whole, the reaction of Dissent to James II's first important overture to the Dissenters was encouraging.

Increasingly, as 1687 proceeded, the king's chief – almost obsessive – aim was to secure parliamentary repeal of the Test Acts of 1673 and 1678. These he saw as the main obstacle to civil rights for Catholics. He was fifty-three years old and aware, at least until his wife's pregnancy was confirmed in autumn 1687, that he was likely to be succeeded by Protestants – William and Mary of Orange – who had made plain their support for the Test Acts as preservatives of the Church of England. However, James seems to have believed that a parliamentary repeal of the statutes would acquire some special permanence and would itself not easily by repealed. He therefore set about recruiting a parliament which would implement his repeal programme. The methods James used to 'pack' parliament were: personal electioneering; manipulation of the power structure in the provinces – especially the lieutenancies and the commission of the peace; systematic canvassing of electors and prospective MPs; and the wholesale reconstruction of town government.

In 1687 James embarked on a personal canvassing campaign to whip up support for his repeal policies. He left Windsor on 16 August on a tour which described a wide arc in the South West, the Welsh Marches, North and South Wales and the Midlands. The tour showed up the continuing support of the gentry for the king's person if not for his policies. James's supposedly curative touching of large numbers of persons for an ailment known as the King's Evil highlighted the mystique of divine-right monarchy. However, far from being an unqualified electoral success, the 1687 tour probably did more harm than good through advertising in the provinces the king's increasingly demonstrative Catholicism. In the great abbey church at Bath, offence was given by James's commissioning a Catholic priest to preach a sermon; in North Wales James prayed for a son at a surviving medieval Catholic pilgrimage site; at Chester he ordered the bishop to find room for Catholic worship; and at Oxford, as we have already seen (p. 56), he tried to bully the fellows of Magdalen into accepting his nominee as president.

James's overhaul of the power structure in the counties was a key element in his electoral strategy. Since the sixteenth century, command of the militia had been in the hands of the chief nobleman in each county, serving as Lord Lieutenant and, in a judicial capacity, as chairman of the county commission of the peace. The system had the advantage of resting the crown's governance of the counties on the firm support of existing social and political structures of local patronage and dependency. In 1687–8 this settled system was profoundly and repeatedly shaken up in displacements and replacements of personnel which seemed to indicate that the king was calling into question the very social hierarchy on which his government ought to rely. Following a grilling of his lords lieutenant in the summer over their willingness to comply with his repeal policy, extensive replacements were carried out. The point to make about these demotions and promotions is not that they were unconstitutional, for they were well within the royal prerogative, but that they were clumsy and bound to cause resentment among the powerful and influential. In counties such as Warwickshire and Shropshire, where Sunderland and Jeffreys respectively were made Lieutenants, promotions were being made of men whose power bases lay at court and in central government rather than in the complex and introverted webs of neighbourliness and affinity that held each of the county communities together.

Two particular appointments to the lieutenancy, both religiously motivated, will show up the king's misjudgment. In Lancashire, the Stanley earls of Derby had ruled the county for the crown since Tudor times; they had even produced a martyr for the royal cause in the person of the seventh earl in 1651. James now replaced the eighth earl by the Catholic Caryll Viscount Molyneux. Molyneux was no upstart; nevertheless, his appointment disturbed the pecking order in the county, installed as the king's representative a man whose regional power base and patronage were doubtful and, worst of all, created a deep sense of grievance in an undeviatingly loyal leading family. Likewise, in the West James chose to replace the Duke of Somerset as Lord Lieutenant of that county with the Catholic Lord Waldegrave. Somerset, who had held Bristol for the king against Monmouth in 1685, was not a man to rebuff in this way. Indeed, no seventeenth-century government, however 'absolute', could afford to antagonize its own nobility. When we come to consider the diffident inaction or the outright hostility of the peerage with regard to James in the crucial autumn of 1688, we may conclude that the king had made a fatal mistake in thus attacking the entrenched power of the magnates.

Below the level of the lords lieutenant were the senior gentry of the shires who served in administrative and judicial capacities as Justices of the Peace, in amateur military capacities as deputy lieutenants and in representative roles as MPs. Typically, they were men of education and public spirit, naturally conservative, basically royalist and Anglican. Their apparently secure hold on the commission of the peace had been consolidated in the nationwide purge of Whigs instituted by Charles II from 1679. Now, though, these men themselves were to be the victims of the large-scale replacement of personnel carried out from October 1686 onwards by a committee chaired by Jeffreys. Out went opponents of James's Catholicizing policies and in their places Catholics and Dissenters were installed. In Lancashire, with its strong Romanist element amongst the gentry, twenty-eight Catholic justices were put on the commission of the peace between January 1687 and mid-1688.

Accompanying the regulation of the counties came an intense campaign to quiz the governing class on their attitude to the king's policies. In autumn 1687 James dissolved his prorogued parliament, first elected in 1685, and on 25 October, in preparation for fresh elections for a new parliament, lords lieutenant were instructed to go down to their counties and canvass all those involved in the electoral process – including deputy lieutenants, Justices of the Peace, sheriffs, mayors, aldermen and town councilmen and government officials – with three questions, concerning: first, their willingness to vote for parliamentary candidates pledged to repeal the penal laws in religion, second, their readiness to stand themselves on that platform, and third, their general views concerning religious toleration.

The answers were by no means as overhelmingly hostile as used to be thought. Purging and replacements in key positions had already taken place; many were basically reluctant to defy the king; and as was indicated by large number of affirmative answers to the third question, asking whether respondents would 'live friendly with those of all persuasions', there was a growing constituency in favour of the basic principles of religious toleration. As with Exclusion, patterns in the returns were regional, with those in agreement with the king – 'consents' – strong in the royalist far North and Welsh Marches. 'The "consents"', wrote Professor J. R. Western, 'seem to have been slightly the largest group and the refusers the smallest . . . the returns provide[d] some encouragement for supporters of the King' (Western 1972). That said, there were problems about the responses, including the large number of ambiguous and evasive answers, the lack of enthusiasm on the part of lords lieutenant and, most seriously, the way the polling process in itself awoke national debate, and thereby opposition.

Included amongst those questioned were mayors and corporations. These were a vital element in James's calculations. The diffidence of the leaders of the traditional landed class, the lords lieutenant, over the three questions, together with the apparent obstructionism of peers such as Somerset, created the opportunity for forming a new social and political alliance between the crown and urban, bourgeois, Nonconformist and, indeed, Whig, elements, laying down the foundations for a new 'synthetic ruling class' (Jones 1970). An important focus of the new alliance would be the corporate boroughs where Nonconformists had their pockets of strength and which returned four-fifths of members of the House of Commons; in them their corporations exercised considerable influence over voting, sometimes in effect nominating their members. The key to control of the corporations was the series of charters issued during the Tory Reaction and giving the crown the right to dismiss members and nominate their replacements. These charters, designed in the earlier 1680s to establish and confirm a Tory and Anglican monopoly of municipal government, were now to be used for the purpose of demolishing that monopoly.

The central government was now about to embark on one of the most drastic assaults on local, specifically urban, government in the country's history. From 14 November 1687 an ambitious nationwide campaign to swing the parliamentary boroughs in the king's favour by introducing Catholics and Dissenters into their corporations was coordinated at the centre by a regulation commission, in which the former Baptist and now Catholic Sir Nicholas Butler played a key role. Active in the ceaseless work of electioneering and information-gathering about individuals and their likely voting was a Catholic lawyer, Robert Brent, in charge of a national team of well-paid agents whose job it was to sound out opinion and cajole voters in the towns. Reconciled Whigs were also to the fore in the campaign, which saw some bewildering changes: Buckingham, for instance, had three new mayors in a matter of months, and Reading no fewer than five 'regulations' – imposed changes of personnel – between December 1687 and August 1688. The government even moved towards an economic and social policy designed to appeal to the pockets of the small businessmen who made up the backbone of the urban Dissenting communities. New charters, as for example at Honiton and Nottingham, might confer significant new economic and marketing advantages on boroughs.

What chance did James's 'synthetic ruling class' have of ruling the towns and of creating a workable electoral front? The answer is that the new political grouping, with crown leadership and central direction, was by no means unviable. In social terms, in towns like Nottingham, growing fast economically, with new Dissenter money and a substantial Nonconformist population, the exclusion of non-Anglican Protestants from the corporation under the terms of the 1661 Corporations Act meant that the municipal governing body did not reflect or represent some of the most important and dynamic elements in the borough's life – elements that were now admitted into the arena of local administration thanks to the king's policy. Nottingham's Presbyterians – some years later said to number 1,400 – were enthusiastic supporters of the Declarations of Indulgence: this was exactly the kind of town and the kind of social stratum in which James's daring socio-political experiment might well have achieved success.

In Norwich, too, by the summer of 1688 the corporation was staffed substantially by members of the city's important Presbyterian community, including men with extensive earlier experience in the council and reflecting much of the city's wealth; if this was a 'synthetic' ruling class in the making, it was by no means ungrounded in wealth and local status. In Bedford, a major Nonconformist centre, members of the Dissenting community were successfully drafted on to the corporation – approaches being made to John Bunyan to serve – but they worked alongside some Anglicans who seem to have been in accord with crown policy. In the North West, especially in the area around Liverpool, Catholicism rather than Nonconformity provided the main alternative to the established Church. In Liverpool itself, leading Anglicans, including James's subservient bishop of Chester, took part in a civic reception for the Catholic bishop, Leyburne. In the north of the county, Lancaster gave a warm welcome to the Catholic judge, Allibone. Thus around the country late in 1687 and early in 1688 there were distinct signs that the attitudes looked for in the king's three questions – respect for other people's religious views, a willingness to see the end of religious repression – were indeed widespread. An address from Coventry subscribed jointly by Anglicans and members of three major Dissenting denominations chimed in exactly with the king's insistence that toleration would 'exceedingly encourage their future industry, to the improvement of trade'.

Optimism at court over the apparent nationwide support for the king's policies needed to be tempered by a realization of what some seemingly tolerant gestures concealed. For example, it might be easy to miss from Coventry's pan-Protestant address any mention of Warwickshire's substantial Catholic population of over 1,000, 6 per cent of the overall population. Liverpool had a trading town's traditions of live-and-let-live and of getting along cordially with neighbouring Catholics as individuals, but this did not extend to accommodating *popery*. Thus the mayor of the borough, which warmly entertained the Catholic bishop, returned on behalf of the corporation a negative answer to the question of a pre-electoral commitment to the repeal of the Test Acts.

Acceptance of a vague spirit of Christian tolerance, then, was one thing, but at the heart of the matter was a widespread wish to keep the Test Acts as an institutional defence of the Church of England against the menace of popery. That message was coming in loud and clear from around the country in 1687–8. Voters in Gloucestershire, for instance, were reported to be 'generally averse to the taking away the Test', while the Justices of the Peace of Merionethshire captured perfectly the anti-repeal viewpoint when they maintained:

> That the Test is a law not to be abrogated, as being the sole support and defence (together with his majesty's gracious assurances of protection) of the established religion and church.

Thus, while many no longer demanded incessant persecution of peaceable Dissenters, Anglicans wanted the Church to be both protected and respected, and James had given an undertaking to that effect at the beginning of the reign. On the face of it, the king had indeed reiterated that assurance in the text of the 1687 Declaration of Indulgence:

> we do declare, that we will protect and maintain our arch-bishops, bishops and clergy, and all other our subjects of the church of England in the free exercise of their religion . . .

However, there would be some who would find even this engagement insufficient. For one thing it did not unequivocally promise full support for the Church as an institution but rather for Anglican clerics and lay people. Indeed, the king's words could be taken as meaning that he saw the Church not as the national establishment of religion but as another voluntary denomination whose members qualified for a kind of toleration and the 'free exercise of their religion'. Furthermore, the king's words could be read as meaning that he did not so much commit himself to upholding the Church as to not attacking it 'by any molestation or disturbance whatsoever'.

However, events in 1687–8 seemed to indicate that a Catholic king had indeed set out to attack the Church of England, and the consequence was the build-up of a volume of resentment against James which formed the background to his fall in 1688. On top of the outrage at Magdalen, he offered licences, one of which was taken up by the vicar of Putney, to allow Anglican incumbents who had converted to Rome to keep their livings. He kept the great primatial see of York vacant from May 1686, giving rise to rumours that he was reserving it for his Jesuit counsellor Fr Petre. However, the clearest evidence of James's offensive against the Church was his Second Declaration of Indulgence, a year after the first.

The bishops' reaction to James's First Declaration of Indulgence had been muted. However, the Declaration of April 1688 contained, as if James really did want to goad the Church leaders, an order that they instruct their parish clergy to read the Declaration from their pulpits on successive Sundays, first in the London area and then throughout the country. The instruction offered a gratuitously unnecessary insult to the Church: for after all, the Indulgence benefited not Anglican parishioners but Dissenters, and it would have made vastly more sense and caused vastly less offence to have had the king's edict read out in the now licensed Nonconformist meeting houses. The order commanding the reading seemed to require the Anglican clergy to act as accomplices in the assassination of their own Church, and it was so damaging to James that Dr Ashley, with no exaggeration, wrote that from it 'can be traced clearly enough the reasons why King James lost his throne'.

7

James's overthrow

The response of the Church leaders to the king's Declaration was to attempt to deflect his policy of overt aggression against the Anglican Church. In May it became apparent that London parish clergy were intending not to read the Declaration and the bishops had a clear responsibility to express the mind of the Church on so grave an issue. On 12 May the unworldly and melancholic Archbishop of Canterbury, William Sancroft, hosted a dinner party for the Earl of Clarendon and a small group of bishops. What eventually emerged from the meeting was a decision to petition the sovereign to be allowed to release the clergy from the obligation to publicize the Declaration. Even this step – modest enough – was not easily taken, for the bishops wanted neither to alienate the Nonconformists by rejecting the Declaration nor to expose the Church to an accusation of disloyalty to the king. However, by 18 May the petition, behind which it is possible to see the hand of Compton, had been signed by Sancroft and six other bishops and was ready for presentation, in a group audience, to the king.

James's unfeigned surprise at the presentation gives the lie to the view that he had issued the Declaration in order to drive a wedge between the Anglicans and the Dissenters; had this been the case, he would have been *expecting* the clergy to reject it. So committed was the king to the policies encapsulated in the now challenged Declaration that, as in the previous September with the fellows of Magdalen, he completely lost control of his temper, telling the bishops that they were responsible for raising a 'standard of rebellion'.

Just how wide of the mark this comment was is revealed in the demeanour, language and indeed in the careers and views of these petitioners. They presented their submission on their knees – and wisely left out of their company Compton, whose presence would have provoked James beyond measure. One of the seven bishops – as surprised by James's reaction as James had been by their petition – captured his colleagues' feelings perfectly: 'We rebels! Sir, we are ready to die at your feet!'. They were simply pleading with the king, in a private audience, 'not to insist upon their distributing' the Declaration. And it was not with their approval that a version of the petition was somehow pirated away and made public through printing. The terms of their brief statement itself also indicates the underlying loyalism of its signatories; their reluctance to comply with the Declaration arose, they said, 'not from any want of duty and obedience to your majesty (our holy mother, the Church of England, being both in her principles and in her constant practice unquestionably loyal)'.

If the words and gestures of the seven were submissive, neither were these men themselves made of the stuff of rebels. They included men like John Lake, Bishop of Chichester, who, evidently stung by the king's blurted-out allegation of stirring up rebellion, retorted, 'Sir, we have quelled one rebellion, and will not raise another' – a clear allusion to his vital role, recognized by James, in holding Bristol against Monmouth. Most members of the group refused the oaths of allegiance to James's successor after his fall. In antagonizing men like this, the king was making the worst mistake a politician can commit – alienating his own natural supporters.

The sequel compounded James's errors. Of all the options open to him, including the issue of a kingly reprimand, he chose the worst, the one most likely to publicize and martyrize the bishops – a full trial on a charge of seditious libel. In the run-up to this, the bishops orchestrated their own heroics beautifully. They refused bail and were put in the Tower, taken there – these somewhat improbable popular heroes – along London's main highway, the Thames, in a blaze of entirely favourable publicity, with 'infinite crowds of people on their knees, begging their blessing and praying for them'. They had become the mascots of anti-popery.

The decision to try the bishops alarmed some of James's advisers; Sunderland, Jeffreys, and even Petre drew back and the Catholic peers opposed prosecution. In fact, this rash move was entirely consistent with the get-tough, hard-man approach that James, who blamed his father's fall and his brother's difficulties on their allegedly soft-centred methods, had determined to adopt; the decision to try the bishops arose from James's own 'pre-possession' [as he put it] 'against the yielding temper which had proved so dangerous to his brother and so fatal to his father'.

The bishops were brought to trial on 29 June 1688. On the face of it, the crown, which controlled appointments to, and dismissals from, the judiciary, should have been confident of a favourable verdict. However, the judges had to keep a wary eye on public, and even more on parliamentary, reactions to their more controversial statements, while the jury was susceptible to public pressure as well as to the daunting presence in court of large numbers of peers in support of the bishops. The bench failed to give the usual clear guidance to the jury, two of the four judges rejecting the charge that the petition was a seditious libel. That, though, was not the central issue: what was at stake now was the wider constitutional question that the seven bishops had raised in their petition when they expressed the view that the king's Declaration was based on an unconstitutional claim to suspend, or dispense individuals from, the laws of the land – in this case the penal religious acts of parliament which the king had abrogated by his unilateral use of the prerogative. The bishops' defence of their Church had turned them into guardians of the constitution which, in turn, protected the subject from absolutism. Had the bishops been convicted of a seditious libel, their claim that the suspending and dispensing powers were unconstitutional would have been rejected by the courts; conversely, the acquittal of the bishops on 30 June was necessarily a verdict against the suspending and dispensing powers, stating in effect that parliamentary statutes could be repealed only by an act of parliament.

Particularly worrying from the king's point of view was the public reaction to the acquittal. Halifax, whose earlier *A Letter to a Dissenter upon Occasion of his Majesty's late Gracious Declaration of Indulgence* had warned the Nonconformists that

71

they were being used by the king to introduce popery by the back door, led the cheering in court. Even more alarming for James, though, was the applause that went up in the great army camp he had established – some thought to over-awe London – at Hounslow Heath. 'So much the worse for them', James remarked gnomically when the cause of the hurrahs was reported to him. But it was so much the worse for him that the army which James had so assiduously been building up since his accession as the ultimate key to his security was evidently riddled with disaffection.

Earlier in the same month had come an event that opened up the possibility of a permanent Catholic dynasty – the birth of a son to James and Maria Beatrice following James's prayers at Holywell in North Wales in the previous September. Before the birth of the prince, James was generally regarded as an ageing man whose pro-Catholic policies would be jettisoned upon his death by his solidly Protestant heirs, William and Mary. The birth of the Prince of Wales destroyed all these optimistic calculations and gave a new urgency to a festering discontent. England would now, surely, have a zealous, Jesuit-educated king for long enough to reverse the Reformation. On 30 June, following the acquittal of the seven bishops, fears for the future of Protestantism induced a group of seven, which included Compton and Danby, to write to the Oranges, whose own hopes of the succession now seemed thwarted by the birth of the prince.

Relations between James and his daughter and son-in-law in the Netherlands had not been running altogether smoothly. Under the impression that they were acting as King Charles would have wanted, William and Mary had shown kindness to Monmouth during his exile, to James's disgust. More recently, James's demand that British regiments in the Dutch service be returned had been regarded in The Hague as a gesture of hostility towards Holland and a sign of increasing friendship towards France; England and The Netherlands were actually drifting towards war. James was dismayed by William's and Mary's unflinching opposition to the abrogation of the Test Acts. A cause of rumbling grievance was suspicion that the Dutch had not done enough to prevent Monmouth and Argyll from sailing in 1685, alongside the fact that the Republic had provided asylum for a number of English political refugees.

It was Orange who delivered the *coup de grâce* to James's

regime in 1688. His intervention was absolutely decisive in as much as the discontent with James's religious policies and constitutional infractions was probably insufficient to topple the king without the impetus of that invasion – though the success of William's bid for power relied on James's unpopularity. Given William's indispensable role, then, it is vital to know why it was that he sailed for England in the autumn of 1688. His decision to act gathered strength in the course of 1688 in view of mounting disaffection in England. His emissaries Dijkveldt and Zuylestein had been testing the English political air and keeping the Stadholder carefully informed. William eventually made it plain that he would not intervene in English affairs without a direct invitation from the country itself, and specifically from high ranking Englishmen – 'some men of the best interest'. That was the significance of the letter of invitation of 30 June which was promptly taken to Orange by Admiral Herbert.

The invitation, wordy and fussily written, offered an analysis of the domestic state of politics in England, emphasizing the grievances which, the signatories promised, would create a favourable climate for the Prince of Orange's arrival:

> The people are so generally dissatisfied with the present conduct of the government, in relation to their religion, liberties and properties . . . that Your Highness may be assured, that there are nineteen parts of twenty of the people throughout the kingdom, who are desirous of change.

However, the invitation's exclusive – and, in the context of the tense international situation in 1688, highly insular – concentration on domestic affairs did not chime in with the Prince of Orange's thinking or the primacy he gave to foreign policy considerations. True, the Stadholder was concerned lest the birth of the Prince of Wales displace his wife in the succession. However, he was also, or more, anxious about James's so alienating his subjects that England would be plunged into a civil war which would rule out any role for the country in Europe, or that James would be politically rescued by Louis XIV and England thereby made one more into a French puppet state. William's intention in 1688 was probably not to depose James but rather to assure England's place in his European schemes: in December 1688 he said that he had no ambition for the English crown.

One of the great peacemakers in European history, albeit through waging defensive war, William was intent in the 1680s on keeping a watch on the Rhine against France. Between the Peace of Nijmegen (1678) and the Truce of Ratisbon (1684), Louis XIV was keeping up intense pressure on the Rhineland corridor, seizing Luxembourg (1681) and Strassburg (1684). William's only hope of containing the insatiable French colossus, which he saw as a threat to liberty, Protestantism, Holland and European security, was to build a ring of steel made up of powers which in combination, but only in combination, might counter the might of France. In the earlier 1680s Austria was preoccupied with holding back the Turks, England under Charles was a French client and the Dutch commercial classes wanted peace and trade with France: William's hope of building his grand alliance seemed remote.

After 1685, though, the European kaleidoscope revolved once more. In Hungary in 1687 eastern Christian states brought to a close the brief Turkish military revival; Austria was now free to resume the defence of the German states on the western front; the Dutch Protestant merchants who dominated the Estates General were now estranged from France by the Revocation of the Edict of Nantes. In 1686 the French threat to western Germany produced the defensive League of Augsburg, an alliance of German princes led by Austria and supported by Spain and Sweden. All that was needed to complete the ring of steel was the inclusion of England, the vital north-western component in the stragetic cordon. England was all the more important to William's strategic considerations in that under James, and for the first time since Cromwell, she had emerged as a significant military power. James was spending around £530,000 a year on the army, compared with his brother's expenditure of about £200,000 and James was also keenly interested in training, drilling and professionalization. There had also been a long-term build-up in the navy, with the total of major vessels doubling between 1660 and 1688. James also took a keen interest in the professionalism and discipline of the royal navy. From the point of view of William's alliance-building, England was now a significant military and naval power in her own right.

William's decision to invade England, then, was heavily driven by foreign policy considerations, while even the timing of his operation was dictated by strategic European thinking, with a French assault on Cologne providing temporary freedom of action in the Channel theatre. John Miller goes as far as to say that 'James's fate was to be decided, not in England but in Paris and The Hague, on the Rhine and on the Danube'. But if this is true, what role did the domestic discontent which the invitation to William stressed play in toppling James? Undoubtedly, there was considerable dissatisfaction around the country from the summer of 1688, as the popular reaction to the acquittal of the seven bishops shows. However, it is very doubtful whether that disquiet would in itself and without an outside encouragement have been sufficient to eject James. His position was relatively strong and the financial provisioning of his state gave particular grounds for confidence: duties on luxury articles such as tobacco, sugar, linen, brandy and fine cloths were comparatively painless and relieved the ruling class of much of the tax burden of the nation. James's annual revenue of £2 million, well exceeded Charles's highest receipts; speaking of 'James's financial triumph', Professor Western wrote, 'The King now had money enough to maintain substantial armed forces and overawe his subjects with them.' Western went on to describe an 'equilibrium' in the country at large: 'The nation had not the means without foreign aid to bring the King to book', and added that James and his Stuart line might have gone on governing in the face of continuing opposition in a situation 'quite normal for what we commonly call absolute monarchs: they would have been powerful but not all-powerful' (Western 1972).

On the one side of the balance was inert disgruntlement veering towards open opposition; on the other a still considerable fund of support, many wishing only for a King James deflected from his Catholic policies. The doctrine of divine-right monarchy was deeply entrenched in public opinion and the fear of civil war was as powerful a dissuasion to opposition in 1688 as it had been in 1681. Both in London and in provincial towns such as Preston there had been official celebrations and services of thanksgiving for the news of the queen's conception. John Evelyn, who attended one of those services, typified royalist and Anglican anti-popery in praying that the king would 'listen to sober and healing Counsels . . .' – that is, return to the Anglican alliance. Yet it was the Prince of Orange who tipped the balance between loyalty and complaint; as Dr Barry Coward writes, summarizing the view of most recent historians: 'There would have been no "Glorious Revolution" without the intervention of William of Orange' (Coward 1980).

William's enterprise of England was his own venture, to which the republican government of the United Provinces gave its consent subject to William's making certain precautions for the safety of the Netherlands in his absence. Some historians have dwelt on the apparent riskiness of the expedition. Professor Kenyon, who describes William's decision as 'little short of mad' and his venture as 'manifestly hopeless', quotes the earlier historian Andrew Browning to the effect that only 'complete confidence' in the absence of resistance or the 'direst necessity' would have drawn the Stadholder's fleet out of Amsterdam. The risks were indeed very grave, not least to Orange himself. Coming in arms, the prince, from the first moment of his landing on English soil would be starring in the role of a foreign invader threatening a civil war – a war which, were he to lose, would almost certainly lead to his execution. Nor was this well-informed statesman likely to have had 'complete confidence' in the absence of resistance or to have been taken in by the easy assurances in the letter of invitation about a mass rising of the people of England in his favour. What Orange had to do, he would have to do largely alone, at least until he had secured sufficient support or complaisance from the English ruling class. It could only have been Browning's 'direst necessity' that led Orange to risk his life in his madcap English adventure. The necessity was that, as developments following 1689 were to show, England, with its treasure and manpower, was the absolutely essential building block in William's grand coalition. In 1688, William of Orange, a Calvinist gambler, a speculator on manifest destiny, ventured at a hazard – and won.

Over the course of the summer, James was receiving information from French intelligence about Orange's military and naval preparations. The king was active in his own army dispositions, while September and October saw a number of initiatives which in effect dismantled the edifice of policies that had given so much offence. In essence, James was moving back towards the Anglican Tories, a political U-turn signalled by his realignment with Sancroft and the rest of the bishops. Talk of a November parliament to repeal the Test Acts was at an end as the king concentrated on military preparations and at the same time awarded the Anglicans and Tories a package of measures that promised to restore much of the honeymoon aura of the Tory Reaction: the Ecclesiastical Commission was suppressed; the fellows of Magdalen were reinstated; London's charter was returned and the other boroughs, after months of confusion and, in some towns, near-chaos, were given back the chartered constitutions they had had even before the Tory Reaction; Catholics were forced to make way for the Tories they had displaced in the commission of the peace and the lieutenancies; and Sunderland, who had converted to Catholicism in order to retain influence over the king, was dismissed.

The political climb-down, whose permanence no one could guarantee, made no difference to the Dutch offensive. After one abortive start, William finally set sail with an army of about 12,000 in an imposing fleet on 1 November. The prince's navy had the best of doubtful autumn weather and winds, passed Dover on the 3rd and landed in the south-west on the 5th, a date laden with Protestant significance. Indeed, the wind as well as the date were soon to acquire a heavy symbolic and providential meaning when it was put about that William had been wafted into Torbay harbour by a 'Protestant wind'. Despite some reservations on Orange's part, the choice of landfall in the West Country, still partly estranged from James by the excesses of the Bloody Assize, and with good access to the capital, was politically as well as strategically sound. A landing in another region much favoured by planners, Yorkshire, would have had the disadvantage of putting the prince in the political debt of the county's leading opposition magnate, Danby.

After the landing, Orange's propaganda machine went into high speed with a conciliatory declaration which listed the errors James had committed at the behest of 'evil counsellors', repeated the doubts that were current throughout the nation about the authenticity of the Prince of Wales as James's son and – a most popular insertion – called for a 'free and lawful Parliament'. Now some of the foremost dispensers of power in the West went over to William, including the Tory former Speaker of the Commons, Sir Edward Seymour, and the Earl of Bath, commander of Plymouth. Elsewhere, aristocratic supporters of William seized the key provincial centres in the North, the Midlands and the East – Chester, York, Hull, Nottingham, Northampton and Norwich.

His army now mounting to a total of 53,000, James, still optimistic (though he had made his will), left London for what should have been the decisive military confrontation with the Stadholder at Salisbury, where he intended to block William's hitherto triumphant progress. We saw (p. 72) that the army at Hounslow Heath reflected at the time of the acquittal of the seven bishops the national mood of suspicion of James's policies – policies which seemed to give, or were portrayed as giving, the green light to the establishment of popery. At Salisbury, the army continued to reflect what was probably the overwhelming national mood of wariness towards James, to the extent of not being prepared to make a firm stand to maintain his position. Between 19 and 24 November, the king watched disaffection in, and desertions from, his *grande armeé*. His health was now broken from the ceaseless anxiety and overwork of the summer and autumn and he was suffering from haemorrhages, exacerbated by the usual botched medical treatment of the period. The show-down with Orange failed to materialize and on 26 November, leaving the army, which was now in increasing numbers leaving him, James retreated to London. He had deserted his own cause and thereby sealed the fate of his dynasty.

It was, however, his dominant sense of family and personal bonds that dictated James's capitulation – the act that made his supplanting inevitable. As Charles I's only surviving son, he had a lively awareness of the acute personal danger posed to himself and his house by a confrontation that he might well lose: in particular, his solicitude for his six-month-old son seemed to argue for escape. Desertions by personal dependants, especially Lord John Churchill, the soldier whose career James had launched, doubled the sense of betrayal that he felt back in London, with the news that his second daughter, Anne, had joined her elder sister against him. Between 8 and 10 December the prince and queen were smuggled out of the country. During December James reviewed his options – military confrontation, negotiation with William, or flight – and, as usual, made the worst choice. He probably hoped, by leaving the realm, to cause the kind of chaos that would force the nation to recall him – on his terms. In point of fact, the prospect of an interregnum and the threat of disorder prompted the nobility and gentry who advised William, now in London, to rally more fully round the prince during December as a focus of stability and order. Anti-Catholic riots in London and the provinces, attacks on property and wild rumours about an Irish army of occupation intensified the need for stability. On William's orders but at the request of the peers, some former MPs and the corporation of London, writs were sent out for the election of a special parliament – a 'Convention' – to meet in January. By Christmas, James had finally left the country and William was left in control. In the following year the king's abdication was consolidated in parliament into a 'glorious' revolution.

8
Conclusion

How had the Revolution of 1688 really come about? Historians often debate the balance between 'personal' and 'impersonal' forces in history – the question of the responsibility for shaping events as between particular individuals and great social forces. To a large extent, the 'Glorious Revolution' was the personal responsibility of two royal individuals. The first was William of Orange. His intervention was absolutely crucial in the deposition of James II. There was considerable dissatisfaction in the country in 1688 with James's policies; these reawoke the nation's fear of 'popery' which we examined at the beginning of this book (pp. 2–4). Throughout his reign, James continued to infiltrate Catholic officers into the army. Yet, while this did not give James a solidly loyal armed force, it had the effect of reawakening in the nation fears of a combination of popery with military rule, while at the same time alienating the Protestant majority of the officer corps and the rank and file, so that when James needed his army most, in November 1688, he found it estranged from him.

The way James's intense campaign of Catholicization in 1687–8 was conducted aroused widespread outrage, seeming to confirm the identification of popery with tyranny. The attack on the fellows on Magdalen College, Oxford, (see above, p. 56) indicated that the king had no respect for tenured rights or corporate privileges. His attempt to 'pack' the House of

Commons suggested that he was prepared to ride roughshod over the freedom of elections and the independence of parliament. His decision to prosecute the seven bishops seemed to give notice of his intolerance of critical advice and his contempt for freedom of speech. Underlying so many of his actions was an entirely erroneous assumption that the oft-proclaimed loyalty of the Church of England implied a supine readiness on the part of its clergy to tolerate any affront to its special status.

Yet, for all the build-up of discontent, it is possible to speculate that James's rule could have survived until his death – had it not been for Orange's invasion. The experience of 1688 was in fact that James could not re-establish Catholicism and that he could be checked in his campaign by methods short of a deposition. The English Catholic community was too small and isolated to partner the king in an attempt to put it at the centre of national life. Vast numbers of conversions to the Catholic faith did not follow from James's brusque efforts to tear down the barriers to equality of opportunity. The case of the seven bishops showed that the king could be opposed without being dethroned. James might have continued to rule a sullen but not insurgent nation. What dethroned James II was Orange's arrival in arms, providing an activating force for what had hitherto been a more inert sense of complaint. Even so, the Stadholder had not come with any specific or announced intention of deposing King James. In the crucial days of December 1688, James, fearful for his and his family's safety yet believing that, by quitting the realm, he could create a power vacuum that would necessitate his recall, took the key decision of the Revolution by abandoning the realm. There *was* no vacuum. Led by the peerage, the ruling class rallied to the Prince of Orange, sealing James's fate.

The role of that governing class – and, indeed, of wider social forces – should be considered in our reconstruction of what happened in 1688. For one further interpretation of James II sees him as a social reformer brought down by entrenched baronial and clerical vested interests. We have seen (p. 59), that as part of his open-door policy towards the largely bourgeois and petit-bourgeois Dissenters in 1687–8, the king was about to introduce a package of economic reforms in the interest of his new social allies, with a preference for trade over land. At the same time, in his attempted political revolution and in alliance with his 'synthetic ruling class', James was threatening to displace the country's traditional social elite of gentry and nobility. The king's punitive measures against leading nobles' infringements of court discipline, no less than his displacement of them in both local and central government in favour of upstarts, awoke their fatal fury. It is highly significant that all the signatories of the invitation to Orange were either nobles or members of noble houses. It is all the more significant that the crucial desertions that initiated James's collapse came from the West Country aristocracy, that the provincial centres were seized for Orange by the Midlands and Northern magnates, and that it was the peerage in London that guided the Stadholder through December 1688. Some might see James as brought down essentially by religious bigotry and the fantasies of mass anti-popery, but the experience of this king, not the first to be crushed in a rising of over-mighty subjects, proves the rule that no seventeenth-century European monarchy was stronger than the landed social and ecclesiastical elite on whose support all government of the day rested and against whose opposition no throne could maintain itself.

Select bibliography

Documents can be consulted in the superb collection of over 400 items edited by Andrew Browning, *English Historical Documents*, vol. VIII (London: Eyre & Spottiswoode, 1951), covering the monarchy and the succession, parliament and its functions, parties, public finance, the Church and its rivals, local government and social life, trade and the colonies, Scotland, Ireland, the armed forces, foreign affairs and key personalities. See also the shorter but very useful volume edited by J. P. Kenyon, *The Stuart Constitution Documents and Commentary* (Cambridge: Cambridge University Press, 1966). Primary sources of great interest and readability for the period include *The Autobiography of Richard Baxter*, edited by N. H. Keeble (London: Dent Everyman, 1985) and Bishop Burnet's *History of his Own Time*, abridged by Thomas Stackhouse (London: Dent Everyman, 1986).

This period is well served by textbooks and collections of essays. Barry Coward's *The Stuart Age: A History of England 1603–1714* (London: Longman, 1980) provides a succinct and informative over-view of the Stuart century. Sir George Clark's *The Later Stuarts 1660–1714* (2nd edn, Oxford: Clarendon, 1988) and David Ogg, *England in the Reign of Charles II* (2nd edn, 2 vols, Oxford: Clarendon, 1934) continue to provide good value. A survey work by a foremost Restoration historian, J. R.

Jones, *Country and Court England 1658–1714* (London: Edward Arnold, 1978) is crisp and informative. J. H. Plumb's brilliant *The Growth of Political Stability in England, 1678–1683* (London: Macmillan, 1967) has had enormous influence on the way that historians have come to look at underlying political and administrative development in Britain in the late-seventeenth and early-eighteenth centuries. Edited by Professor Jones, *The Restored Monarchy 1660* (London: Macmillan, 1979) includes articles on the crown, the parties, the Church and foreign affairs. Collected essays edited by Tim Harris, Paul Seward and Mark Goldie, *The Politics of Religion in Restoration England* (Oxford: Basil Blackwell, 1990) feature works on Danby; the bishops and the Whigs; 'Exhuming the Popish Plot'; and London radicals and revolutionary politics, 1675–1683, along with important studies of regional politics.

For the Plot, which triggered the whole crisis of the late 1670s and early 1680s, see the fast-paced account by J. P. Kenyon, *The Popish Plot* (London: Heineman, 1972). J. R. Jones untangles the politics of the Exclusion Crisis in *The First Whigs* (London: Oxford University Press, 1970). In *London Crowds in the Reign of Charles II: Propaganda and Politics from the Restoration until the Exclusion Crisis* (Cambridge: Cambridge University Press, 1987), Tim Harris draws our attention to the strength of demotic Toryism. A masterly survey of politics and government between Exclusion and the Revolution is J. R. Western's *Monarchy and Revolution. The English State in the 1680s* (London: Blandford, 1972).

The explosive issue of Catholicism is examined in John Miller, *Popery and Politics in England 1660–1688* (Cambridge: Cambridge University Press, 1973), while Douglas R. Lacey deals with the politics of Nonconformity in *Dissent and Parliamentary Politics in England, 1661–1689* (New Brunswick, NJ: Rutgers University Press, 1969). The third volume of Richard L. Greaves's majestic trilogy on the radical tradition in post-Restoration Britain is *Secrets of the Kingdom: British Radicals from the Popish Plot to the Revolution of 1688–9* (Stanford, CA: Stanford University Press, 1992).

For this period dominated by issues of personality, good

biographies abound. Understandably, the figure of Charles II attracts attention, with Maurice Ashley's *Charles II* (London: Weidenfeld & Nicolson, 1971); R. Hutton's *Charles II: King of England, Scotland and Ireland* (Oxford: Clarendon, 1989) – see also his excellent *The Restoration* (Oxford: Oxford University Press, 1985); J. R. Jones's *Charles II: Royal Politician* (London: Allen & Unwin, 1987); and John Miller's massive *Charles II* (London: Weidenfeld & Nicolson, 1991). James II has been studied by F. C. Turner, *James II* (London, Eyre & Spottiswoode, 1950) and more recently by John Miller in *James II: A Study in Kingship* (Hove: Wayland, 1978). Two other classic political biographies are K. H. D. Haley, *The First Earl of Shaftesbury* (Oxford: Clarendon, 1968) and J. P. Kenyon, *Robert Spencer, Earl of Sunderland* (London: Longmans, 1958).

A useful introduction to the Continental background comes in J. R. Jones, *Britain and Europe in the Seventeenth Century* (London: Edward Arnold, 1966). In his brilliant *Revolution and Empire Politics and the American Colonies in the Seventeenth Century* (Manchester: Manchester University Press, 1990), Robert M. Bliss considers the links between English and colonial politics.

For the reign of James II and the Revolution, David Ogg's *England in the Reigns of James II and William III* (Oxford: Clarendon, 1955) remains a powerful narrative. John Childs, *The Army, James II and the Glorious Revolution* (Manchester; Manchester University Press, 1980) is important on the military dimension. J. R. Jones provides a fine account of the Revolution in *The Revolution of 1688 in England* (London: Weidenfeld & Nicolson, 1977). W. A. Speck has contributed the highly readable and informative *Reluctant Revolutionaries: Englishmen and the Revolution of 1688* (Oxford: Oxford University Press, 1988).